SUCCESS AND DYSLEXIA

Sessions for coping in the upper primary years

Nola Firth and Erica Frydenberg

ACER Press

First published 2011
by ACER Press, an imprint of
Australian Council *for* Educational Research Ltd
19 Prospect Hill Road, Camberwell
Victoria, 3124, Australia

www.acerpress.com.au
sales@acer.edu.au

Text © Nola Firth and Erica Frydenberg 2011
Design and typography © ACER Press 2011

This book is copyright. All rights reserved. Except under the conditions described in the *Copyright Act 1968* of Australia and subsequent amendments, and any exceptions permitted under the current statutory licence scheme administered by Copyright Agency Limited (www.copyright.com.au), no part of this publication may be reproduced, stored in a retrieval system, transmitted, broadcast or communicated in any form or by any means, optical, digital, electronic, mechanical, photocopying, recording or otherwise, without the written permission of the publisher.

Copying of the blackline master pages

The purchasing educational institution and its staff are permitted to make copies of the pages marked as blackline master pages, beyond their rights under the *Act*, provided that:

1. The number of copies does not exceed the number reasonably required by the educational institution to satisfy its teaching purposes.
2. Copies may be printed from the CD supplied, but these should not be altered by electronic/digital or other means.
3. Copies are not sold or lent.
4. Every copy made clearly shows the footnote ('*Success and Dyslexia* © Nola Firth and Erica Frydenberg 2011').

For those pages not marked as blackline master pages the normal copying limits in the *Act*, as described above, apply.

Edited by Holly Proctor
Cover design, text design and typesetting by ACER Project Publishing
Printed in Australia by BPA Print Group

National Library of Australia Cataloguing-in-Publication entry

Author:	Firth, Nola.
Title:	Success and dyslexia : sessions for coping in the upper primary years / Nola Firth, Erica Frydenberg.
ISBN:	9781742860190 (pbk.)
Notes:	Includes bibliographical references.
Subjects:	Dyslexia--Treatment--Handbooks, manuals, etc.
	Dyslexic children--Handbooks, manuals, etc.
Other Authors/Contributors:	Frydenberg, Erica
Dewey Number:	616.855306

This book is printed on paper derived from well-managed forests and other controlled sources certified against Forest Stewardship Council® standards, a non-profit organisation devoted to encouraging the responsible management of the world's forests.

Foreword

Children with learning difficulties do not leave their problems in the classroom; their struggle to master literacy skills pervades many aspects of their lives and can impact on their social interaction with peers, their self-confidence and self-esteem, and their attitudes to learning. Many of these children develop maladaptive strategies to draw attention away from their difficulties. Some withdraw from learning and social situations, while others – especially boys –tend to act out because it is better to have classmates laugh at your antics than because you can't read or spell.

Children who do not acquire literacy skills in the early years of school will often continue to struggle academically. Over time, they may develop negative attitudes towards learning which further compromises their progress. Some become alienated from school and leave at the earliest opportunity, but with diminished life chances; their poor literacy skills limit their career choices while years of failure and loss of self-esteem will inevitably affect their outlook on the world.

Ideally children with learning problems will be picked up in the early years of school, appropriate assessment will be organised, and an individualised intervention plan implemented. The earlier this help is provided, the better the chances that the child will succeed; as time goes on the more difficult and costly intervention becomes. Unfortunately, too many children do not receive the help they need, either because the necessary resources are not available, or because their problems are subtle and only become apparent in later grades.

Learning difficulties are common – as many as 15 per cent of children are said to have some school problems. There are a variety of causes including intellectual disability, developmental delay in one or more areas of development, problems with language or memory, attentional or behaviour problems, and lack of learning opportunities in the years before school. The term 'dyslexia' is sometimes (erroneously) used to describe *all* children with learning difficulties, but actually is used more appropriately to categorise a smaller number of children who have a learning disability that is neurologically based, likely to be genetic in origin and lifelong, and difficulties that are resistant to change irrespective of the help they receive. Because these children usually have normal intelligence, their lack of progress is particularly frustrating to them and to their families, and can be a source of confusion for teachers. It is no wonder then, that after a few years at school, they have often developed coping strategies which can be maladaptive and make it even more challenging for them to make progress at school.

Success and Dyslexia has been written to help teachers and students overcome some of the negative attitudes and behaviours that can be associated with dyslexia, though it can also be used for all students who struggle at school, whatever the causes. Based on sound theoretical principles, and supported by research as to its efficacy, the program is designed to be incorporated into the curriculum and the culture of the school to help them address the needs of children who are struggling. It focuses on three areas of functioning: coping awareness, positive thinking and assertiveness. The authors state that the program 'teaches young people to be aware of and take control of how they cope with learning difficulties. Students learn to think positively by challenging self-defeating thoughts, discovering what they want, and asking for that appropriately.'

The book, with its accompanying CD, is designed as a universal (whole-class) coping program with additional components that are undertaken by those students who have dyslexia. It has been tailored for students in the upper primary years as this is when they tend to be forming coping strategies, and, as the authors explain, it's critical that these strategies are positive in preparation for the transition to high school. It contains detailed guidelines for classroom teachers, together with case vignettes that demonstrate successful implementation approaches. The carefully structured sessions provide explicit instructions, are multimodal so as to minimise the need for student reading and writing, and provide opportunities for revision and reflection.

The introduction includes very useful information on how schools can support students with dyslexia, ranging from characteristics and behaviours that might offer early clues as to diagnosis, through to creating a 'dyslexia friendly' school environment and very detailed suggestions for providing support for students in the classroom. Then follows a well-organised, straightforward and practical series of steps for making a difference for students with dyslexia.

Teaching is not the same as learning. Many children, including those with dyslexia, have barriers to achieving literacy that make it very challenging for them and for their teachers alike. It is too easy for us to conclude that it is all too difficult, that it is unrealistic to expect all children to achieve academic success, and that some are destined to have problems despite our best efforts. Nola Firth and Erica Frydenberg have produced a resource for schools and for teachers that deserves widespread uptake. Grounded in sound theory and arising from a solid body of research in cognitive behavioural therapy, it is not a magic bullet that will enable children with dyslexia to overcome the underlying learning disabilities. Rather it is a practical program that teaches them coping strategies and assertiveness, promotes positive thinking, and builds resilience. Teaching children these concepts will assist them to make the most of the strengths that every child has, and increase the likelihood of setting them on a developmental trajectory that leads to positive outcomes throughout their lives. It will also help to create an educational philosophy and school culture that does not give up on any child, no matter what barriers to learning he or she faces.

Professor Frank Oberklaid AOM, MD, FRACP, DCH
Foundation Director,
Centre for Community Child Health
The Royal Children's Hospital, Melbourne

Contents

Foreword	iii
List of handouts	vii
Acknowledgements	viii
Introduction	1
Theory and research	2
Supporting students who have dyslexia	5
Guidelines for using this manual	9
Part 1: Coping awareness and goal setting	**15**
Sessions 1–5: Guidelines for teachers	16
Session 1: What is coping?	22
Session 2: How do you cope?	24
Dyslexia support group: Link to Sessions 1–2	30
Session 3: Your coping profile	32
Dyslexia support group: Link to Session 3	33
Session 4: What's your goal?	35
Dyslexia support group: Link to Session 4	37
Session 5: Choose clever coping	38
Dyslexia support group: Link to Session 5	42
Part 2: Positive thinking and problem solving	**43**
Sessions 6–7: Guidelines for teachers	44
Session 6: Choose powerful thoughts	48
Dyslexia support group: Link to Session 6	52
Session 7: Problem solving	53
Dyslexia support group: Link to Session 7	54
Part 3: Assertiveness and program finalisation	**55**
Sessions 8–11: Guidelines for teachers	56
Session 8: Why be assertive?	60

Session 9: Assertive language — 69
Session 10: Assertive body messages — 72
Dyslexia support group: Link to Sessions 8–10 — 74
Session 11: Revision and finalisation — 76

Bibliography — 79
Resources – General — 82
Resources – Dyslexia — 84

List of handouts

Handout 1: 'How Do You Cope Profile' 27

Handout 2: How to cope with achieving your goal 40

Handout 3: Can you keep your balance? 63

Handout 4: Reasons, feelings and consequences for assertion, aggression and passivity 64

Handout 5: Scenario examples for assertion practice 65

Handout 6: Assertive, aggressive or passive? 66

Handout 7: My Bill of Rights 67

Handout 8: How do you feel? 68

Handout 9: Say what you want 71

Handout 10: Completion certificate 78

Acknowledgements

We gratefully acknowledge the significant contribution to this project of Professor Lyndal Bond. Her input regarding implementation of mental health programs in schools, as well as her statistical expertise, was invaluable. We also acknowledge the support of The Cass Foundation that enabled adaptation of the program in response to feedback from earlier research, and of the Australian Research Council that enabled the implementation of the program to be evaluated. Finally, we appreciate the support and interest over the last six years of the many teachers and students who were involved in the development and trial of the program. We cannot hope to name them all but would like to mention in particular two of these teachers, Marita Nicholas and Andrew Bridge, who gave so very generously of their time, energy and expertise.

INTRODUCTION

Taking control in the tough times

Success and Dyslexia is an evidence-based program that assists upper primary students, especially those who have dyslexia, to increase their ability to take control of and cope well with the problems that occur in their lives.

Underpinned by cognitive behavioural principles, *Success and Dyslexia* concentrates intensively on three skill areas: coping awareness, positive thinking and assertiveness. The program teaches young people to be aware of and take control of how they cope with learning difficulties. Students learn to think positively by challenging self-defeating thoughts, discovering what they want, and asking for that appropriately. They practise these skills within the framework of individually nominated personal goals.

Taking control of coping with dyslexia

Success and Dyslexia is unique in that it is designed for use by students who have dyslexia. It is now known that adaptive coping with dyslexia is a more powerful predictor of life success than the extent of the dyslexia (Margalit, 2003). In addition to literacy programs and inclusive learning environments, programs are therefore needed that specifically target resilience for those who have dyslexia. *Success and Dyslexia* addresses this need by teaching these skills within the context of a universal (whole-class) coping program. It includes 10 additional, concurrent sessions for students who have learning disabilities, including dyslexia. Within the context of this smaller group situation the strategies and ideas from the whole-class coping program are reaffirmed and built on in relation to coping with dyslexia. While appropriate for all students, all components of the program use best practice for students who have dyslexia. This includes explicit strategy instruction, relevance to students' personal lives, opportunity for revision and generalisation, and print-free activities.

Theory and research

Success and Dyslexia has been extensively trialled in schools and adapted in response to teacher feedback.[1] When implemented with fidelity to the manual guidelines, the program is likely to assist all students, including those who have dyslexia, to develop more effective coping and to feel more in control and a greater sense of well-being (Firth, 2009).

Needs of upper primary age students

The program has been especially tailored for upper primary school students. Students at this age are developing their coping strategies, so this is an ideal time for them to learn about helpful ways of coping. The students are old enough to understand the coping concepts and thus have the opportunity to learn positive coping strategies before they undertake the challenge of transition to secondary school. Because it is designed to be both intensive and focused, the program allows for in-depth learning and reinforcement, both of which are necessary for generalisation and integration into students' daily lives.

Whole-school change and adaptability to the unique needs of each school

Programs need to be integral to the priorities and needs of each particular school if they are to be effective and sustainable (Firth et al., 2008). *Success and Dyslexia* is therefore nested in a whole-class, whole-school approach and the program has been designed to have a core structure and process, with activities that can be chosen and adapted to meet the needs of individual schools and students. The ease with which the *Success and Dyslexia* program has been integrated into the school curriculum in the research phase of the program reflects the success of this innovative, nested, inclusive model that involves all students, including those who have dyslexia.

Dyslexia: Definitions and prevalence

In Australia, there is confusion regarding the terms dyslexia, specific learning difficulties, learning difficulties, specific learning disabilities and learning disabilities (Louden et al., 2000). In this program the term dyslexia is used and refers to Australian definitions recorded by the recently formed National Dyslexia Working Party (2010), the National Health and Medical Research Council (1990) and the Australian Temperament Project (Prior, 1996).

---

1 A substantial component of the research was supported by the Australian Research Council Grant no DP0877877, Frydenberg, Bond, (Firth).

Students who have dyslexia as referred to in this program have neurological processing problems that are likely to be genetically based and lifelong, and are highly resistant to change despite excellent teaching. Because these problems are independent of intelligence they may be experienced by students at all levels, including those who are gifted. These students have significant difficulty (e.g. are two years or more below the expected level for their age) with reading, spelling or mathematics and have associated processing problems, such as difficulty with phonic analysis or auditory short-term memory. Their difficulties are not caused by intellectual disability, visual or hearing problems, Asperger's syndrome, lack of opportunity or emotional difficulties unrelated to dyslexia. Diagnosis is usually carried out by an educational psychologist, but teachers can begin the process by using norm-referenced educational tests (see page 5, 'Supporting students who have dyslexia').

Whilst estimates vary according to exact definition, researchers on the Australian Temperament Study found that approximately 10 per cent of people are affected (Prior, 1996). A recent investigation into dyslexia in primary schools in the United Kingdom reported estimates between 6 and 8 per cent (Rose, 2009).

Taking personal control

Feeling in control is known to be an important factor for all students in overcoming difficulty (Shapiro & Astin, 1998). It is a key factor in whether or not an individual chooses effective coping strategies (Perez & Reicharts, 1992) and is also important for academic success (Dweck, 2000).

Success and Dyslexia teaches personal control both directly and through development of skills and strategies. Students are taught directly that an attitude of taking control in the face of difficulty is likely to be helpful in dealing with the problem. They are also taught directly the need for responsible choice of strategies, and of the ineffectiveness and likely harm of using strategies such as self blame. The program enables students to see that there are many ways of coping with difficulty and that they can choose coping strategies according to their individual need. Completion early on in the program of the *Adolescent Coping Scale 2nd edition* (Frydenberg & Lewis, 2011) or the 'How Do You Cope Profile' (see *Handout 1*) gives students access to awareness of their current coping methods.

Positive thinking, assertiveness, goal setting and problem-solving strategies help students to gain control over their feelings and actions when things are difficult. Positive thinking involves understanding the link between self-talk and feeling, and learning to challenge negative self-talk that exaggerates difficulty. Students are taught to recognise and challenge negative self-talk, and to replace it with more realistic and encouraging self-talk.

Goal setting, problem solving and assertiveness convey to students that they can work for positive change when things are difficult. These strategies assist students to respond to difficult situations as more of a challenge and less of a threat and they encourage choice of productive coping strategies such as working on the problem, rather than using strategies such as self-blame or worry.

Personal control and coping with dyslexia

Despite skilled teaching, those who have dyslexia rarely learn to read and write with ease (Shaywitz, Morris & Shaywitz, 2008). Dyslexia is known to be a major source of stress (Nalavany, Carawan & Rennick, 2011) and is associated with negative life outcomes such as:

- passive learning styles (Núñez et al., 2005)
- depression (Sideris, 2007)
- disruptive behaviour in school (Chan & Dally, 2000)
- school drop-out (Deshler, 2005)
- social isolation (Bryan, Burstein & Ergul, 2004)
- juvenile delinquency (Svetaz, Ireland & Blum, 2000)
- unemployment (Prior, 1996).

Many people are successful despite their dyslexia. It is the way people cope rather than the extent of the dyslexia that has the greatest influence on outcomes (Margalit, 2003). Well-known examples include the actor Tom Cruise, businessmen Richard Branson and Kerry Stokes, Australian sailor and youngest person to circumnavigate the globe, Jessica Watson, Australian writer and comedian Catherine Deveny, Australian writer of children's and gardening books, Jackie French, and Carol Greider, Nobel Prize winner in medicine in 2009. Taking control and using helpful, proactive coping strategies are the keys to success for such people in spite of their continuing difficulties with reading, spelling and mathematics (Goldberg et al., 2003; Reiff, Ginsberg & Gerber, 1995).

However, although taking control is likely to be helpful for students who have dyslexia, these students are known to be at risk of ignoring their problems, giving up (Firth, 2009; Lackaye et al., 2006) or being disruptive in class (Chan & Dally, 2000). *Success and Dyslexia* directly addresses these issues and teaches students the strategies used by successful people who have dyslexia.

Program content and process

The content and presentation of *Success and Dyslexia* is grounded in research-based best practice and is designed to enable optimum access by all students, including those who have dyslexia. It is clearly structured, includes explicit instruction of the helpful and unhelpful strategies, provides frequent opportunity for revision and reflection, requires little student reading or writing and incorporates multi-modal learning. Naturalistic circumstances, high student motivation, strategy instruction and sufficient self-reflection, revision and practice opportunity are known to be necessary to achieve mastery and generalisation of strategies, and this is especially the case for students who have dyslexia (Fensham, Gunstone & White, 1994; Firth, 2001b; Gresham, 1998; Purdie & Ellis, 2005; Westwood, 2001). To achieve this, the program has incorporated use of personalised goals, role-play practice of a small number of specific strategies and concepts, and use of print-free mediums. The positive cognitive restructuring and assertion in the program are specifically included to counter the passivity and learned helplessness that is a known risk for students who have dyslexia (Firth, 2009; Nunez et al., 2005). These components give access to increased internal control (positive thinking) and increased external control (assertiveness). Assertiveness training has also been successfully trialled with students who have dyslexia (Firth, 2001b).

Program evaluation

Several studies have been conducted, and continue to be conducted, to evaluate the benefits of the program. Generally the process of evaluation involves pre- and post- measures such as the *Adolescent Coping Scale 2nd edition* (Frydenberg & Lewis, 2011) and the perceived control section of the *Arc's Self-Determination Scale* (Wehmeyer & Kelchner, 1995). Qualitative data, such as interviews with teachers, have also been regularly used. Reported findings concern students who had dyslexia and undertook the program, compared to students who had dyslexia but did not undertake the program. Findings for students who undertook the program included increased sense of control and higher use of adaptive coping strategies, such as working hard and focusing on the problem (Firth, 2009). More recent findings include both students who have and do not have dyslexia. It is highly recommended that an evaluative component be included in each implementation. Evaluative tools can include those mentioned above and others that are deemed to be appropriate, including asking participants to describe what they have learned and what they are doing differently.

Supporting students who have dyslexia

The *Success and Dyslexia* program is designed to explicitly teach students to be resilient in the face of the challenges that dyslexia brings. Teachers also need to dispel any confusion about the problems these students face and ensure these students experience success. The following section presents some brief guidelines for dyslexia diagnosis and whole-school and classroom support (see also the Resources – Dyslexia section of this manual for further information).

Diagnosis

It is important to obtain an informed diagnosis of dyslexia. Reversal of letters and other commonly identified 'signs' are not necessarily indicators. Manifestation of dyslexia can vary in extent and kind from person to person and many other possible causes of difficulty with literacy or mathematics may need to be eliminated.

Teachers need to be alert in the first two years of school to early indicators of possible dyslexia (e.g. phonic analysis difficulties and difficulty remembering lists). Some children can be slow to begin to acquire these skills but this does not necessarily mean they have dyslexia. Lack of response to good literacy and maths teaching in the early years is, however, one indication of possible dyslexia.

By about Grade 2 level, normed educational tests (e.g. phonic analysis, spelling, oral comprehension, reading comprehension and mathematics) will be helpful in clarifying the extent of any difficulty the student is experiencing. If a child is older, a review of their school report history will also be helpful, as it will show whether literacy difficulties have been ongoing. If, despite extra literacy or mathematics support, a child has ongoing, significant (e.g. two or more years below the norm) difficulty with reading, spelling or maths, diagnostic referral is appropriate. The following characteristics, while not always present, should also be noted as possible indicators of dyslexia:

- a discrepancy between oral and reading comprehension
- a discrepancy between oral and written expression
- a discrepancy between understanding of mathematics concepts and execution of algorithms
- a dislike of reading and writing
- ongoing difficulty spelling commonly used words (e.g. 'were' or 'what')
- difficulty with isolating sounds and syllables in words
- difficulty remembering non-phonetic sequences of letters (e.g. in non-phonetic words such as 'through' or 'many'), mathematics tables, spelling rules, or sequences for solving maths problems
- messy handwriting
- low self-esteem and/or disengagement from school.

Formal diagnosis is usually undertaken by an educational psychologist and involves elimination (or identification) of other possible causes of literacy or mathematics difficulties. These include vision, hearing, speech development difficulties, intellectual disability, Asperger's syndrome, emotional difficulties or lack of opportunity to learn. The diagnosis usually includes the *Wechsler Intelligence Scale for Children* (Wechsler, 2003), administered by an educational psychologist, as well as normed educational tests if results are not already available.

A professional diagnosis reveals a child's individual strengths and difficulties and forms the basis for an informed and effective response plan. This is likely to decrease confusion by all concerned (student, teacher and parent) and helps to maintain the student's self-confidence and ability to make a proactive and resilient response to their situation. Additionally, 'learning differently' is an accepted disability under the Australian *Disability Discrimination Act 1992* and these students have a legally supported right to equal access to educational opportunities. Professional, documented assessment such as that outlined above forms part of the evidence for eligibility for the extra support needed to achieve equal access to educational opportunities (e.g. use of computer software and extra examination time).

A 'dyslexia friendly' school environment

In addition to resilience programs and informed diagnosis, students who have dyslexia need to be supported within a 'dyslexia friendly' school environment that facilitates a resilient response. Such support includes:

- a whole-school dyslexia policy that is included in school policy documents (e.g. teaching handbooks and welfare policy)
- systematic assessment and monitoring processes in place that ensure teachers know who in their class has dyslexia
- professional development for staff about dyslexia support
- parent information seminars on supporting children with dyslexia. See *Life Success for Children with Learning Disabilities* (Raskind et al., 2003, p. 106, see Resources – Dyslexia).

For more information on 'dyslexia friendly' schools see the British Dyslexia Association's *Dyslexia Friendly Quality Mark for schools* (see website in Resources – Dyslexia), and the Churchill report titled *To Assess Resilience Programs for Children who have Specific Learning Disabilities* (Firth, 2010, see Resources – Dyslexia).

Dyslexia support in the classroom

Within a 'dyslexia friendly' school environment as outlined above, students who have dyslexia need to receive best practice mathematics and literacy teaching including explicit instruction in phonic analysis. Despite this support, progress in those areas is likely to be varied and, for some of these students, quite slow. In addition to the resilience teaching that is the main focus of this program, the following classroom teaching strategies are also needed (see also Resources – Dyslexia):

- detailed awareness of, and response to, the individual characteristics of each student who has dyslexia (e.g. ensuring students with high oral comprehension receive high

level information by non-print mediums; and speaking and writing in short sentences for students who have short term memory problems)
- modification of assignments/homework/tests to ensure students who have dyslexia can experience success (e.g. increased time allowance and decreased length with focus only on areas of highest priority)
- student access to information and expression via non-print or low-print means. This may include:
  - use of mp3 players/podcasts to support access to written information
  - low-print handouts (e.g. key points underlined, dot points, mind maps rather than paragraphs)
  - student access to, and guided use of, assistive technology (e.g. text-to-speech and speech-to-text software and predictive typing)
  - student presentations via non-print means (e.g. use of mind maps, drama, PowerPoint slides or video)
  - use of a scribe or reader
  - posting information in advance on the school website (e.g. homework, assignments and reference material) to give opportunity for students to pre-read and for parents and other helpers to participate; and text-to-speech capability also installed on the website
- separation of assessment into content and presentation (with only the latter addressing spelling accuracy)
- regular positive feedback that precedes negative corrections (e.g. noting the number of words spelled correctly as well as those needing correction)
- regular revision opportunities (e.g. use of key points summary displays at the beginning and end of each lesson, provision of regular revision assignments)
- pairing or grouping students so they can share strengths and ask for help (e.g. some students assisting with reading and spelling and others providing ideas or artwork); this may also involve taking time to teach students the skills of working in groups
- development of strong partnerships with parents including a home/school communication system
- creation of an inclusive classroom environment where difference is expected and valued (e.g. open discussion of dyslexia within the class, invitation of speakers who have dyslexia and who have made a success of their lives)
- heightened awareness and speedy response to any bullying or other discrimination towards students who have dyslexia
- teaching of social skills to students who have dyslexia and who are not well integrated into the class groupings
- showcasing and building on the areas of strengths shown by students who have dyslexia.

Guidelines for using this manual

Program overview

This program involves a universal (whole-class) coping program and an additional and concurrent dyslexia coping program that is undertaken by the students who have dyslexia. It is divided into three parts: Coping awareness and goal setting (Sessions 1–5); Positive thinking and problem solving (Sessions 6–7); and Assertiveness and program finalisation (Sessions 8–11).

Each part has an introductory section containing guidelines for teachers and a vignette that illustrates ways in which teachers have successfully implemented the part.

The universal (whole-class) program includes:

- awareness of personal coping style (using the *Adolescent Coping Scale 2nd edition* or the 'How Do You Cope Profile' in *Handout 1*)
- exploration of a variety of coping strategies and styles
- goal setting and problem solving in relation to goals chosen by each student
- positive self-talk strategies
- assertive communication strategies.

The dyslexia support components include:

- direct teaching of the importance for successful outcomes of taking control of responses to dyslexia
- development of self-awareness of current coping approaches to having dyslexia
- presentation of successful dyslexia role models
- opportunity for individual investigation of dyslexia
- discussion of dyslexia-related issues in a supportive group
- opportunity to receive individualised support for a dyslexia-related goal
- assertion and positive thinking skill reinforcement in relation to a dyslexia-related goal
- reinforcement of *Success and Dyslexia* skills and strategies within the regular classroom environment.

The dyslexia support components are linked to each session, located in close proximity to the sessions to which they are linked and are in boxed, italic text. They are also available as a PDF document on the accompanying CD.

It is important to ensure that students receiving the dyslexia support components also experience the universal (whole-class) program.

Sequence and timing

The sessions are presented in a sequence that allows a foundational introduction of the concepts of coping, followed by choice of personal goals and then strategies of positive thinking and assertion to use in relation to the goals. The sequence has been found to work well, although the positive thinking and assertion sections may be interchanged. The duration of most sessions is a minimum of one lesson of 50 minutes to introduce the concept. Several lessons can then be used for the reinforcement activities. Timing will depend on the activities chosen.

The vignettes

Each of the three parts of the program contains a vignette as part of the introduction. The aim of these vignettes is to illustrate successful outcomes that can occur for individual students who undertake the program and to also demonstrate implementation approaches that have been observed to be particularly successful. The vignettes are drawn from real life but names have been changed and some case studies used in the vignettes have been amalgamated.

Key messages to share

Each session has a 'Key messages to share' section. These contain brief, key messages for each session that are important for students to receive and understand.

KEY MESSAGES TO SHARE

What is assertiveness?
- *Assertiveness* is standing up for yourself and solving your own problems without hurting other people. It is being in control of yourself, taking account of your needs and the other person's needs.
- *Aggressiveness* is trying to get what you want by attacking someone. It often shows you have lost control of yourself. The other person's needs are not taken into account.
- *Passiveness* is not standing up for yourself when someone hurts you. It is not taking control of the situation and your needs are not taken into account.

Examples

Some sessions contain 'Examples' for use in the session.

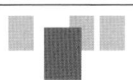

> **EXAMPLE OF AN ASSERTIVE DYSLEXIA REQUEST**
>
> When you ask me to read out loud in front of the class, I am embarrassed. I would like not to have to do that in public.

Reminders

Some sessions contain 'Reminders' that remind teachers of important implementation issues.

> **! REMINDER**
>
> Read aloud each item to accomodate any students who have reading difficulties.

Activities

Each session has 'Activities' for working with the concepts. These activities support and reinforce the session's core structure and purpose, and can be chosen and adapted to meet individual school and student needs. Teachers thus have the opportunity to decide on the type of activities that will best fit their classes and the extent of reinforcement they are able to promote. Such reinforcement, both at initial teaching and afterwards, will assist students to adopt and internalise the concept and skills. Relating the concepts and skills to other activities, both in and out of class, will be invaluable in helping students to internalise them and use them regularly in their daily lives.

All resources suggested for use in the 'Activities' or other sections of the program are referenced in the sections: Resources – General; Resources – Dyslexia.

Resource lists

In addition to the bibliography there are general resource and dyslexia-specific resource lists titled respectively, Resources – General and Resources – Dyslexia. These lists are included both in the manual and on the CD.

The CD

The video on the accompanying CD can be used by teachers to inform and inspire students in a learning capacity. It contains conversations with authors, teachers, parents and students, as well as classroom footage demonstrating the program in action, a student role play and pertinent facts. Resource lists, reproducible handouts and the support group sessions are also provided. Their availability on the CD is denoted in the manual by the following symbol:

The video footage focuses on a group of Year 6 students at Wedge Park Primary school, Melbourne, Australia, who participate in the dyslexia support group sessions. Of these 10 students, four have been formally diagnosed by professionals as having dyslexia, and the remaining six have been assessed by teachers at the school as having strong dyslexic tendencies. The parents of these children have provided permission for their participation in the program and in the video.

The coping profile

Success and Dyslexia has been developed for use in conjunction with the *Adolescent Coping Scale 2nd edition* (Frydenberg & Lewis, 2011). The ACS–2 gives an in-depth and psychometrically validated measurement of coping. Its 20 conceptual areas of coping provide a powerful framework and language that assists individuals to explore their coping choices and options. As an alternative, a simple coping profile, the 'How Do You Cope Profile', has also been included (see *Handout 1*) along with background material about 'The coping concepts' (see page 25).

Further reinforcement

Success and Dyslexia introduces students to the concepts, language and skills of effective coping. Further reinforcement three months, six months or a year later will also help students to build on this coping foundation. Complementary programs have been developed for secondary school use, some of which could be used as extension activities or once students reach secondary school. These include: *Best of Coping* (Frydenberg & Brandon, 2007), the companion CD-ROM, *Coping for Success* (Frydenberg, 2007, see Resources – General) and *Think Positively: A Course for Developing Coping Skills in Adolescents* (Frydenberg, 2010, see Resources – General). Opportunity for such reinforcement and development is known to increase long-term behaviour change (Gresham, 1998).

Inclusion and class climate

An important component of the program model is that it is inclusive. All students in the grade take part in learning how to cope well with learning difficulties, and the students who have dyslexia complete extra sessions and activities to focus these skills on their situation of having dyslexia and the particular challenges this brings. It is important that the students who have dyslexia take part in all the main class coping sessions, and that the work for the whole class and small group are integrated. To achieve the latter the dyslexia support group and whole-class teachers need to communicate frequently and support each other.

It is essential also that a classroom environment is established, both in the whole class and in the dyslexia support group, where students feel relaxed, safe and free to disclose only what they feel comfortable to share. Especially in the dyslexia support group, confidentiality needs to be established at the outset such that all students know that information shared in the group must not become public.

The classroom environment for the whole class and dyslexia support group needs to be a place where:

- teachers model positive thinking, assertive behaviour and acceptance of learning differences
- teachers are aware of and responsive to individual student needs
- teachers demonstrate confidence in their students' ability to take control, rather than being aggressive or passive when things get difficult
- difficult feelings can be safely aired
- students are expected to use positive thinking and assertive behaviour in the classroom
- there is opportunity for students to have a say in classroom events and decisions
- students are encouraged and expected to support each other.

Part 1:
Coping awareness and goal setting

Sessions 1–5

Guidelines for teachers

Coping awareness (Sessions 1–3, 5)

The initial part of the program enables young people to look at and reflect upon the coping strategies they are currently using when faced with difficult situations. After an introduction to the concept of coping, students construct their own individual profile of their coping strategies. They then reflect on and discuss a variety of coping strategies with a view to increasing their ability to achieve the most positive outcomes in difficult situations.

The term 'coping' refers to the responses, that is, the thoughts, feelings and actions, that individuals make when dealing with stressful situations in everyday life. Research about coping has shown that it is possible for young people to become aware of the coping strategies that they are using and to learn to use more effective strategies more frequently and decrease the use of less effective ones. They can also learn new strategies that they had not previously considered. Students also learn the language of coping and this gives a shared and positive way of talking about dealing with stress.

There are innumerable responses young people have when faced with difficulty, but the coping measures used in this program are based on common coping responses used by thousands of young people. Young people's responses differ according to their personality, gender, age and the situation that they are dealing with. There are no right or wrong responses but, rather, what is helpful and what is not helpful (see Frydenberg, 2008 for a comprehensive review of research on adolescent coping). However, while many of these responses may be effective depending on the situation, some of them are more likely to be associated with negative outcomes. The responses in the coping measures used in this program that are more likely to lead to positive outcomes and development of resilience in the face of difficulty include:

▸ focusing on the problem and working hard on it
▸ thinking positively about the situation
▸ sharing the problem with helpful people
▸ meditation and/or prayer
▸ relaxation and physical exercise.

Responses that are more likely to lead to low energy and negative outcomes include:

- self-blame
- worry
- giving up
- ignoring the problem
- always keeping problems to oneself.

Taking responsibility and control and acting from a positive position to try to change or work through a difficult situation is more likely to lead to a positive outcome than being withdrawn, worried and/or blaming oneself or others. This still applies if the situation involves adapting to something that cannot be changed, such as being born with dyslexia.

We also know that lower academic achievement and school disengagement are likely to be associated with the less productive strategies listed above. It is therefore important for young people to realise that these strategies are often a source of anxiety, depression, stress, distress, exaggeration of the problem and an inability to concentrate. With support and a willingness to change, use of these non-productive coping strategies can be reduced or replaced by a more productive repertoire.

Goal setting (Session 4)

The process of individualised goal setting is introduced early in the program to allow sufficient time for students to achieve their goals. If students are encouraged to use the insights from the program to pursue their individually chosen goal their motivation for the program is also likely to increase.

Goal setting involves taking an active and responsive position, rather than a passive or reactive position. The process assumes both responsibility and empowerment. It involves using proactive coping strategies to plan, anticipate and prevent problems from occurring. Proactive copers build up their resources and their activities are purposeful.

It is important that time and support is given to guide students through this process of setting goals. Where possible the goal needs to be chosen and owned by the student rather than provided by the teacher. Students may need teacher suggestions but if they are to own the goal and be motivated to achieve it, the final choice needs to be made by the student. Each goal needs to be specific, measurable and realistic in order for the students to have optimum opportunity of achieving their goal. It is also important that there is regular follow-up, encouragement and guidance for each student regarding progress with their goal. If students achieve one goal, or if their original goal becomes impossible, they can be encouraged to set a new one.

Viraj's story

Viraj, a student in Grade 6, started the year getting into fights with other students. His responses in class were usually articulate and insightful in spite of his untidy writing, low written output and frequent spelling mistakes. He also read slowly and with difficulty. In maths sessions he had trouble remembering tables and algorithm sequences. His class teacher, Lexi, found it difficult to get Viraj to focus and reported that he avoided work that he found difficult. She said she felt concerned and frustrated about his lack of progress in reading and writing, especially as in lower grades he had completed small group literacy classes.

Following consultation between his parents and teachers, Viraj obtained an assessment by an educational psychologist and was diagnosed as having dyslexia. His performance on oral comprehension and non-verbal concepts was reported as a little above average for his age. His ability to analyse words into sounds and syllables (phonological analysis) and to recall unrelated pieces of information (short-term auditory memory) was, however, significantly below average for his age.

Viraj's mother said that while she felt anxious about his future she was relieved when they received the diagnosis because she knew there was a problem and at last they all knew what it was. She added that she thought Viraj was also relieved because, 'He knew at last he was not dumb'. The diagnosis was especially interesting to Viraj's father as he also had had a similar history of difficulty with spelling and reading and now suspected that 'after all this time' he may have found the reason why.

Lexi remarked that she thought that Viraj's parents were relieved after the diagnosis because they now had a reason for what was happening and they knew that they did not need to blame themselves, or the teachers, or Viraj himself and they could instead move ahead in an informed way.

Lexi also reported that she found it very helpful to have diagnostic information about Viraj's difficulties. She began immediately to ensure that Viraj and some other students who had literacy difficulties had priority access to the computers in the classroom and encouraged them to use the spell checker when they wanted to write. Lexi also gave Viraj a daily, explicit program on phonic analysis in addition to the daily class literacy program. Finally, all students in her class, including Viraj, were encouraged to present their assignments in their preferred mode. For example, this might include an oral presentation using PowerPoint slides, videos, or graphic representations with low writing content.

Lexi also made sure the *Success and Dyslexia* program in her class was given a high profile. Parents were kept up to date about the program via the school newsletter and were encouraged to reinforce at home the strategies learned by the children. She posted attractive, colour-coded signs on the wall containing the lists of productive and non-productive coping strategies with green for 'productive' and red for 'unproductive'. Nearby were displays of student-generated examples of some of these strategies. For example, relaxation included going for a swim, playing with your dog and listening to music. These displays were referred to during class when difficulties arose. Lexi recalled such a discussion:

> So you say, well, you know you chose it, you chose a red one that we've already decided is not the most positive. How about you look at the green poster and tell me one you could have chosen on the green side.

Lexi also constantly reminded her students, both as a group and individually, to be proactive, to persevere and to find ways around difficulty, and she praised use of any such strategy when it occurred.

Viraj took part in the whole-class coping program as part of his normal class schedule, where he completed his individual coping profile. He also agreed to take part in the additional dyslexia support group sessions. These were taught by Jim, a senior teacher, who knew the students well. The support group was chosen according to who had dyslexia and was therefore made up of students of widely varying ability.

At first, along with another boy in the class, Viraj did not appear very engaged with the activities in the dyslexia support group. Unless reprimanded, he giggled, poked his partner, and sometimes bumped and rocked the table.

Jim took the time to discuss the coping profile privately with Viraj. Viraj's profile showed high use of self-blame and worry, and medium use of ignoring the problem and keeping problems to himself. Jim suggested other more positive responses that might be available to him, such as relaxation and 'hanging in there' even when it was 'tough going'. Using a new colour, Viraj superimposed his preferred coping strategies on his profile. He chose to decrease self-blame and increase focusing on the problem and relaxing.

After a couple of sessions, once Jim had successfully established a respectful and fun atmosphere in the small group, Viraj began to settle, open up and share his uncomfortable feelings with others when he couldn't spell or read well. Most of the group acknowledged similar feelings and Jim discussed how it was normal to feel stress and important to choose good ways to cope with it. He gave examples of his own experience of stress and how he dealt with it.

Viraj set two goals for himself, one in the whole class and one in the dyslexia support group. In the whole-class coping program he set a goal of responding calmly even if he was angry. After discussion with Lexi he made the goal more specific so that it was limited to school time only and he developed a strategy of thinking of a peaceful place to imagine when he felt upset. Lexi told him she thought his goal was a hard one. 'What if someone pushes you over?' she asked. The other students in the class suggested that he ask his friends to help him walk away. Other strategies they suggested for dealing with anger included talking to your dog, hitting a pillow, singing and using stress balls. However, Lexi made sure she left the final decisions to Viraj regarding his goal and how to achieve it.

In the dyslexia support group sessions, Viraj set a goal to increase his spelling score by two levels on the normed midyear spelling test that was taken by all of Grade 6. He planned to practise his spelling regularly to achieve this. Jim suggested that this goal might be too high. He encouraged Viraj to ask his class teacher, Lexi, for a realistic and exact level to aim for. Jim also talked about the need to practise. He reminded them that champion tennis player, Roger Federer, would not have achieved success in his sport otherwise. Under Jim's direction Viraj also made a graph to measure the progress of his goals. He recorded the number of times per day when he felt he had achieved his goal of responding calmly.

Jim and Lexi ensured that the whole-class and dyslexia support group coping program components were coordinated and integrated. They had regular communication about Viraj's and the other dyslexia support group students' progress and Lexi ensured these students had time at the end of each day to fill in their goal graph. At the beginning of each of the support group sessions, Jim enquired about Viraj and the other students' goals. The students contributed ideas to help Viraj with his goal and Jim pointed out and praised Viraj for times he'd seen him responding calmly or heard from Lexi that he had done so. Viraj also was invited to help Jim install speech-to-text software on the class computers. When technical problems occurred with this software, Jim modelled being open about his feelings of frustration and perseverance and his coping strategy of asking for help.

As the program progressed, the coping language became regularly used in Lexi's classroom. Lexi felt it was especially useful as it replaced the language of 'bad' behaviour. Once when she became angry at a student he asked her what coping strategy she was using!

By the end of the program Viraj told the small group that he was sometimes able to respond more calmly to frustrating situations. Jim verified for him that Lexi was also witnessing his progress in this regard. Lexi reported that Viraj was keen to use the computer and that he was willing to present information publicly to the class. Viraj's score on the spelling test increased a little, but in contrast to some of the other students who had similar goals (which they achieved), unfortunately Viraj did not reach the spelling level he had aimed for. Jim discussed dealing with such disappointments with the students in the dyslexia support group. He pointed out that spelling was an area that was particularly difficult to change for people who had dyslexia. He emphasised that the development of the skill of recovering and finding a new way forward or a new way around the difficulty was essential.

By the end of the program all agreed that Viraj had increased his confidence. Viraj himself, when asked about the program, said, 'I learned that there is quite a lot of ways of solving a problem'. Lexi indicated that she felt Viraj was less hard on himself now he knew what was actually happening to him. She said he's 'heaps more positive in his work, will have a go, is writing more and practising more and is positive. [He] is editing his work much more'. She also said he had more friends now as the other boys were happy for him to be part of their group. She added that she felt happier now that she understood what Viraj was dealing with and felt she had been able to assist him rather than asking him for the impossible. Viraj's parents also reported that he was more comfortable with himself, less angry, and more able to ask for help and to work to find ways around difficult situations.

Session 1

What is coping?

Aims

- To introduce the idea of coping.
- To discuss making good coping choices.
- To explore a variety of ways of coping.

Session sequence

1. Share with students the purpose of the program and a brief outline of what it involves.

   KEY MESSAGES TO SHARE
   - The purpose of the program is to give students more control over their thoughts and actions when things are difficult.
   - Taking personal control is known to be associated with social and academic success.

2. Discuss the meaning of coping and stress.

   KEY MESSAGES TO SHARE
   - Coping is what you do in any situation which may or may not be difficult.
   - Stress is the body's response to a difficult situation.

3. Discuss choosing good ways of coping either to solve a problem or to calm down.

Activities

- Read aloud from a book to introduce the idea of stress and how some people cope with stress. Possible books include:
  - *I Had Trouble Getting to Solla Sollew* by Dr. Seuss
  - *I Got a D in Salami* by Henry Winkler and Lin Oliver
  - *Oh The Places You'll Go* by Dr. Seuss
  - *Franklin in the Dark* by Paulette Bourgeois and Brenda Clark (see Resources – General; Resources – Dyslexia).
- Ask students what situations they find hard to deal with. For example:
  - not being invited to a party
  - their parents divorcing.

> **REMINDERS**
> - Don't ask students who have trouble reading to read aloud in front of the class.
> - Read aloud all written material in the program to accommodate any students who have dyslexia.

Session 2

How do you cope?

Aims

▶ To complete the *Adolescent Coping Scale 2nd edition* (Frydenberg & Lewis, 2011) or the 'How Do You Cope Profile' (see *Handout 1*) in order to create individual coping profiles.

Materials

▶ The *Adolescent Coping Scale* questionnaire (or the 'How Do You Cope Profile'). See page 12 for information on the more comprehensive *Adolescent Coping Scale*.

Preparation

▶ Read 'The coping concepts' on the opposite page.

Session sequence

1. Remind students of the idea of coping and choosing good ways of coping either to solve a problem or to calm down.
2. Explain that the profile will show them how they cope when things get difficult. Reassure them that there are no right and wrong ways to cope, but that everyone can learn new ways and have more control when things are difficult.
3. Distribute the *Adolescent Coping Scale* or the 'How Do You Cope Profile' and read out the instructions.
4. Assist students to complete the scale profile.

> **REMINDER**
>
> ▶ Read aloud each item to accommodate any students who have reading difficulties.

The coping concepts[2]

We all cope in different ways and generally tend to use some coping strategies more than others. Twenty commonly used strategies are listed below. These are then grouped in two basic styles of coping.

Commonly used coping strategies

1. *Seek social support* – sharing the problem with friends or relatives so they can listen and/or help you to deal with it.
2. *Focus on solving the problem* – tackling the problem by learning about it and working to solve it.
3. *Work hard and achieve* – applying yourself and putting in all your efforts to succeed.
4. *Worry* – being concerned about the future.
5. *Invest in close friends* – relying on a close friend or relationship.
6. *Act up* – making yourself feel better by taking it out on someone.
7. *Wishful thinking* – hoping that things will turn out well.
8. *Social action* – letting others know about the concern and getting support by writing petitions or organising a meeting.
9. *Tension reduction* – trying to make yourself feel better by doing something to release tension.
10. *Not coping* – not doing anything that helps deal with the problem.
11. *Ignore the problem* – trying to block out the problem.
12. *Self-blame* – when you see yourself as responsible for the problem.
13. *Keep to self* – withdrawing from others and trying to keep them from knowing about concerns.
14. *Seek spiritual support* – praying and/or believing in assistance from God or a spiritual leader.
15. *Focus on the positive* – having a cheerful or positive outlook about the situation.
16. *Seek professional help* – going to a qualified person for help, like a teacher or counsellor.
17. *Seek relaxing diversions* – doing things to relax (other than sport).
18. *Physical recreation* – playing sport; keeping fit.
19. *Humour* – entertaining others, making fun in difficult situations.
20. *Accept best efforts* – accepting that you have done your best and therefore there is nothing further to be done.

---

2 Adapted from Frydenberg, E. & Lewis. R. (2011). *Adolescent Coping Scale* (2nd ed.). Melbourne: ACER Press.

Coping styles

The strategies can be grouped in two basic styles of coping:

Style 1: Productive coping
This style includes strategies which work on solving a problem while remaining optimistic, fit, relaxed and socially connected.

Style 2: Non-productive coping
This style includes strategies that are largely negative and avoid the problem.

Handout 1: How Do You Cope Profile

Complete the 'How Do You Cope Profile'.

1. Think about how you mostly cope with your problems.
2. Colour in the box which shows how often you use the coping method.
3. Create your profile line by joining the coloured boxes. See the example below.

Name _____   Date   /   /

Coping method	Don't use	Use a little	Sometimes do this	Often do this
Work on solving the problem				
Work hard				
Worry				

Success and Dyslexia © Nola Firth and Erica Frydenberg 2011

Coping method	Don't use	Use a little	Sometimes do this	Often do this
Work on solving the problem				
Work hard				
Worry				
Wishful thinking/ daydreaming				
Ignore the problem				
Blame yourself				
Keep the problem to yourself				
Think on the bright side				

Success and Dyslexia © Nola Firth and Erica Frydenberg 2011

Coping method	Don't use	Use a little	Sometimes do this	Often do this
Relax				
Give up				
Play sport or do exercise				
Share the problem with friends/parents				
Reduce tension (e.g. cry or scream or do risky things)				
Pray/meditate				
Ask for help from a teacher or doctor				

Success and Dyslexia

Dyslexia support group

Link to Sessions 1–2

Aims

- *To establish the dyslexia support group.*
- *To relate the idea of stress and coping to that of coping with dyslexia.*
- *To introduce the idea of coping well with dyslexia.*

Session sequence

1. *Welcome students and establish a safe, structured class climate by discussing class rules and need for confidentiality, mutual sharing and support (see also 'Inclusion and class climate' notes on p.13).*
2. *If the group is newly formed, do some warm-up activities to build trust. Examples might include: asking students to line up in order of their ordinal position in the family; asking each student to tell two truths and a lie and the group deciding which is the lie; trust games such as blindfolding and guiding a partner through an area 'mined' with paper plates.*
3. *Revise the idea of stress and coping. Share that* Success and Dyslexia *aims to help students have more control over their thoughts and actions when things are difficult, especially when the difficulty is due to spelling, reading or maths problems. Give a brief outline of what will happen during the dyslexia support group sessions component of the program.*
4. *Share with students that most people who have dyslexia find it a major source of stress, but there are many people who are very successful despite having dyslexia. For example, Tom Cruise, Richard Branson and Jessica Watson.*
5. *Ask students to share difficult times that have happened because they have dyslexia. Ask them to say what they did to cope and how they felt.*
6. *Read from stories by Henry Winkler and Lin Oliver such as* I got a D in Salami *(see Resources – Dyslexia). The lively stories are about Hank Zipzer, a student who has learning disabilities/dyslexia. Note that Henry Winkler has dyslexia himself and is also a successful actor and writer.*

7. *Share with students that research results show that most successful people who have dyslexia understood they had dyslexia and then, despite their difficulties with reading, spelling and/or maths, took control by using clever coping methods (see 'Key messages' below). Also, see/read out to students from* Life Success for Children with Learning Disabilities: A parent guide *(Raskind, et al., 2003, see Resources – Dyslexia). Tell students that taking part in this program will help them to learn to use these methods.*

   KEY MESSAGES TO SHARE

   Clever coping with dyslexia involves:
   - accepting and understanding your own dyslexia
   - being aware of and managing your feelings
   - asking for help
   - setting goals
   - thinking up clever ways around problems (e.g. a lawyer in one study admitted that he sometimes left his office and rang to ask someone how to spell a word; no one in the office knew he did this)
   - persevering even when it is difficult.

8. *Share with students that many people with dyslexia also learn positive things from having dyslexia (e.g. understanding others' difficulties and how to help them, and how to keep going despite difficulty). See also* Learning Disabilities and Life Stories *(Rodis, Garrod & Boscardin, 2001, see Resources – Dyslexia).*

Session 3

Your coping profile

Aims

▶ To create individual coping profiles.

Materials

▶ *Adolescent Coping Scale 2nd edition* Long Form Score Sheet and Individual Profile chart or the 'How Do You Cope Profile' (see *Handout 1*).

Session sequence

1. If using the 'How Do you Cope Profile' begin the session at Item 3. If using the *Adolescent Coping Scale* hand out the Long Form Score Sheet and Individual Profile chart. Explain, read and demonstrate all sections of the Score Sheet and Individual Profile chart. Suggestions for this step:

    ▶ Demonstrate how to complete the profile on an overhead slide or whiteboard.
    ▶ Provide calculators to assist with calculations.

2. Assist students to plot their results on their profiles. Complete profiles for any students who have difficulty.
3. Make time during the class (or at another time) to talk individually with each student about their profile and their coping choices.

Activities

▶ If using the *Adolescent Coping Scale* this session could be part of a maths class about calculator use, multiplication or graph construction.

Dyslexia support group

Link to Session 3

Aims

▶ *To help students understand the way they cope with their dyslexia.*
▶ *To provide models of successful coping with dyslexia.*
▶ *To give individual attention to students who need assistance completing the profile.*
▶ *To give students the opportunity to understand their own situation with regard to dyslexia.*

Session sequence

1. *Read aloud the strategies on the profile (especially if using the* Adolescent Coping Scale 2nd edition). *Remind students that focusing on and working on problems created by having dyslexia is the way to achieve success. Blaming themselves (e.g. calling themselves stupid), worrying or ignoring the problem do not help and are likely to undermine them and decrease their opportunity to succeed.*
2. *Help students who have difficulty with maths or spatial relations to complete their coping profile. Complete it for them if necessary.*
3. *Discuss privately with each student how he or she copes with dyslexia. Refer to their coping profile.*

Activities

▶ *Redo the 'How Do You Cope Profile' (see* Handout 1*) or the* Adolescent Coping Scale *with students, answering the questions only in relation to their dyslexia.*
▶ *Invite a speaker who has dyslexia to speak to the students/teachers/parents. Give the dyslexia support group time alone with this person.*
▶ *Establish mentoring relationships between each student and a successful adult or successful secondary school student who has dyslexia.*

- *Complete a dyslexia self-awareness project where each student investigates their own dyslexia situation, including their strengths and difficulties. This could be by reference to their files and/or by asking teachers, parents and clinicians. Outcomes could include:*
    - *a poster, play, or oral presentation that shows what each student can do well, what is difficult and how he/she learns best*
    - *a presentation, using PowerPoint slides, to students in a lower grade who have dyslexia on how to cope with their situation*
    - *becoming a mentor for a younger student who has dyslexia and teaching that student to also understand their dyslexia including how they learn best and how they can cope with their dyslexia situation.*

Session 4

What's your goal?

Aims

- To enable students to choose personal goals to work on during the program.
- To teach students how to set and work towards goals.

Session sequence

1. Ask students to choose two areas that they would like to cope with more effectively in their lives.
   - One goal is to be about schoolwork.
   - Goals need to be achievable by the end of the *Success and Dyslexia* program.

   > **KEY MESSAGES TO SHARE**
   >
   > Encourage students to choose goals that:
   > - are related to something they *really* want and that they are prepared to work hard to achieve
   > - are realistic, i.e. not too big
   > - are exact
   > - include a date
   > - are recorded in some way.
   >
   > For example, 'My goal is to learn to jump my horse over a three-tyre barrier within six weeks'.

2. Invite students to share their goal with the group if they are comfortable doing so.

> **! REMINDERS**
>
> ▶ Help students individually with their progress towards their goal. Regular personalised assistance and support from teachers in regard to this element of the program is critical. It will help students use the *Success and Dyslexia* strategies both in and out of the classroom. Success in achieving their goal will increase students' belief in, and motivation to learn, the program strategies.
> ▶ Remember to:
>   ▷ regularly ask students individually about their goal progress
>   ▷ help them to recognise their progress
>   ▷ encourage perseverance when things are difficult
>   ▷ help students find ways to overcome goal obstacles
>   ▷ help students reframe goal strategies and goals if current ones are not successful or practical.

Activities

▶ Lead students in a relaxation session and ask them to visualise themselves enjoying working towards and then achieving the goal. See *Relaxation for Children* (Rickards, 1994, see Resources – General).
▶ Have a goal display wall. Ask students to draw pictures/symbols or take photos to show their goal.
▶ Share and discuss literature (stories, poems, films) that show people working towards and achieving goals. Discuss the steps they took in order to succeed. A book that presents an excellent coping role model especially for students who have dyslexia is *Screw It, Let's Do It* by Richard Branson (2006, pp. 40, 52, Resources – Dyslexia). Read the brief stories by Richard about how he coped with difficult challenges when he was young.

Dyslexia support group

Link to Session 4

Aims

▸ To assist students to set achievable goals that are related to coping with their dyslexia.

Session sequence

1. Help students to set their individual dyslexia goals. Encourage them to use specific, achievable goals for issues related to their academic work and to choose goals that they really care about.
2. Ensure students have recorded the goals they have chosen. This can be in pictorial or other form.
3. It is essential to give regular individual attention to each student who has dyslexia and to help him or her with ways to move towards their goal. Be ready to help students acknowledge their own efforts and progress. Students who self-blame or are negative thinkers may discount their own efforts and progress.

Activities

▸ Read from Screw It, Let's Do It by Richard Branson (2006, p. vii) and discuss with the students what they think of how he sets his goals and whether any of them have similar stories to tell (see Resources – Dyslexia).
▸ Begin each dyslexia support session by making time for group members to report on their goal progress. Ask the group to give each other helpful feedback about how to remove obstacles to achieving goals.

Success and Dyslexia

Session 5

Choose clever coping

Aims

▶ To revise and further explore ways of coping well.

Session sequence

1. Discuss the advantages and disadvantages of different ways of coping (refer to the coping profiles and use some of the activities below).

   KEY MESSAGES TO SHARE

   ▶ Different coping methods work for different situations.
   ▶ It's important to be flexible and have many different coping methods you can use.
   ▶ Some methods, depending on the circumstances, can be unhelpful. For example, ignoring the problem, keeping the problem to yourself, giving up or taking drugs.
   ▶ Self-blame and worry are known to be ineffective and sometimes harmful because:
      ▷ they are an attack on yourself
      ▷ they leave you with no energy to solve the problem.

   ! REMINDER

   ▶ If using the *Adolescent Coping Scale 2nd edition*, read aloud the definitions and examples of the strategies on the Individual Profile chart.

Activities

▶ Students colour code the strategy symbols on *Handout 2: How to cope with achieving your goal* to show which strategies they will choose to use and which they will avoid for

each of their personal goals. In particular, remind students about the need to avoid self-blame and worry. Invite students to share their choices with a partner or the group. Note that the useful strategies of positive thinking and assertively working on the problem will be discussed in future sessions.
- Students blow up a balloon and write on it a self-blaming thought they have in relation to one of their goals. They then jump on the balloon to remind them not to self-blame.
- Lead students in a relaxation exercise to help them to recognise where in their bodies they feel tension and worry (see Rickards, 1994, see Resources – General). Have students colour in the bodily feelings accompanying the feeling of self-blame and/or worry (see *Handout 8: How Do You Feel?*).
- Show a film or read a story of an example of a person who has used a helpful or an unhelpful coping strategy. Discuss the situation, the response and the result.
- Discuss ways of coping with difficult situations that students have experienced or are likely to experience.
- Students form small groups and make a video of group members discussing how they have used a strategy and how useful it was. See the *Coping for Success CD* (Frydenberg, 2007, see Resources – General) for examples. Show the video to other classes.
- Students create a story/poem/play/artwork (individually or in groups) about the way a character coped with a situation and what the consequences were. Share and discuss.
- Set up an internet chat forum to discuss progress with home practice of goals and coping choices.
- Corner card game:
  1. Make cards of different ways of coping (see examples in the booklet *Enhancing resistance 2* available on the Mindmatters website (see Resources – General)).
  2. Students choose or are randomly assigned a card.
  3. A difficult situation is presented by a class member or teacher.
  4. Students hold their card up and choose a corner according to whether they think, for that situation, the way of coping on the card is:
     a) Useful
     b) Harmful
     c) Not much use, but not harmful
  5. Students discuss why they chose the corner.
- Extension activities for good readers/writers. For examples see *Coping for Success CD* (Frydenberg, 2007), *Best of Coping* (Frydenberg & Brandon, 2007) and *Think Positively: A Course for Developing Coping Skills in Adolescents* (Frydenberg, 2010). See Resources – General for details of these titles.

Success and Dyslexia

Handout 2: How to cope with achieving your goal

Name _____

Instructions: Using the key for each goal (see below), tick the coping methods you will choose as most useful for each of your personal goals. Then put a cross against those you will choose to work to avoid.

Goal key:

Goal 1 ◯   Goal 2 ☐

Helpful strategies

Relax	Think on the bright side
Play sport or do exercise	Work on solving the problem
Work hard	Pray/meditate

Success and Dyslexia © Nola Firth and Erica Frydenberg 2011

Coping awareness and goal setting

Share the problem with friends/parents	Try to belong in your group
Ask for help from a teacher or doctor	Get up a petition

These strategies may be less helpful. Worrying is not helpful. Self-blame is definitely harmful.

Worry	Keep the problem to yourself
Wishful thinking/daydreaming	Ignore the problem
Give up	Blame yourself
Reduce tension (e.g. cry or scream or do risky things)	

Success and Dyslexia © Nola Firth and Erica Frydenberg 2011

Dyslexia support group

Link to Session 5

Aims

- To revise the 'Key messages to share' from Session 5.
- To encourage students to use helpful coping strategies in relation to their dyslexia goals.

Session sequence

1. Remind students to choose coping strategies that are used by successful people who have dyslexia.
2. Advise against using self-blame, worry or ignoring the problem.

> **! REMINDERS**
>
> Clever coping with dyslexia involves:
> - accepting and understanding your own dyslexia
> - being aware of and managing your feelings
> - asking for help
> - setting goals
> - thinking up clever ways around problems
> - persevering even when it is difficult.

Activities

- Screw It, Let's Do It by Richard Branson (2006, pp. 40, 52) presents a good coping model for students who have dyslexia (see Resources – Dyslexia). Read the brief stories about how he coped with difficult challenges when he was young.
- See the many activities in Life Success for Children with Learning Disabilities: A Parent Guide (Raskind et al., 2003, see Resources – Dyslexia).

Part 2:
Positive thinking and problem solving

Sessions 6–7

Guidelines for teachers

Positive thinking (Session 6)

The use of positive thinking as a coping strategy is underpinned by cognitive behaviour therapy, a psychological approach concerned with identifying the role of our thoughts and their effect on how we feel and what we do. Cognitive behaviour therapy has been used successfully with a variety of groups, including children. Positive thinking involves understanding the link between self-talk and feeling, and learning to challenge negative self-talk. This gives students a way to take control over their internal reactions to stress and to thus be in a position to focus on the problem and work hard to achieve positive change.

Self-talk is a term used to describe the thoughts that we generate to explain to ourselves things that are happening around us. Our feelings are controlled by this self-talk, and are not entirely dependent on what is happening in our world. This is a powerful position as it is possible to be aware of and choose what we think, and this in turn can change how we feel and then act.

In this component of the program students are taught to recognise and challenge negative self-talk and replace it with more realistic and encouraging self-talk. They are also taught to see a difficulty as a challenge, rather than one of threat or harm.

Negative self-talk involves exaggeration and overgeneralisation in response to difficulties. Instead of containing a difficulty to a particular situation and time, it is seen as generalised over all areas of life and lasting forever. Such thinking is counterproductive and is associated with low self-esteem, anger and frustration with oneself and others, as well as depression, poor health and poor performance. Negative thinking is not usually accurate and is likely to lead to feelings of hopelessness and a lack of energy to work to make positive change. Conversely, positive self-talk is likely to lead to feeling hopeful, energised and able to focus on dealing effectively with difficult situations.

Young people need to first become aware of what messages they are saying to themselves and then learn to challenge any negative messages they are using. This doesn't mean pretending not to be disappointed or hurt about situations. It means accepting such feelings, but challenging negative interpretations of what has happened to see whether they are true, and then substituting a more positive interpretation.

Habits of negative self-talk include: putting oneself down (e.g. 'If I failed this spelling test I must be stupid'); overgeneralising in the face of a setback in one area (e.g. 'Everybody hates me', or 'I never get it right'); ignoring or discounting positive experiences as luck (e.g. 'It was lucky I passed that test'); jumping to negative, worst-case scenario conclusions without evidence (e.g. 'I don't know anyone there. I'll have a really rotten time').

If they are to thoroughly learn and internalise awareness and challenge negative thought habits, students will need frequent opportunities to practise this skill. Although the technique is introduced in one session (Session 6) in the *Success and Dyslexia* program, it will need to be frequently reinforced using the extensive activities provided for this session. Application in relation to the individual goals for the *Success and Dyslexia* program will also motivate students to generalise the skill to life outside school. Opportunities to revisit the skill regularly in class will also be important, as will teacher modelling.

Problem solving (Session 7)

This session is devoted to revising coping skills and positive thinking skills, to revisiting goals and helping students solve associated problems. Regular personalised assistance and support from teachers in regard to helping students with their goal progress is critical to the success of the program. The goals enable students to use the program strategies in the context of something they personally value. Success in achieving these goals will thus increase belief in, and motivation to use, the strategies in the future.

Students who tend to think negatively may need their progress drawn to their attention. If they have made little progress this is an excellent opportunity to refer them back to the coping strategies available to them as well as to the need to use positive thinking to maintain hope and energy. This session also contains a problem-solving process that students can use to overcome obstacles to achieving their goals. This process is a way of using the strategy of focusing on and working hard on the difficulty. Students may, however, also need assistance to change or modify their actual goal if the current one is not practical. If they have already achieved their goal a new one can be set.

Harriet's story

Before the program began Harriet was likely to be looking around and talking with other girls in class, playing with her hair ribbon, or spending a long time ruling margins rather than beginning to work. Harriet's Grade 6 teacher, Steve, found that when she did begin to write, it was a slow process and she would highlight any words she thought might be spelled incorrectly.

In the dyslexia support group Harriet set herself a goal of being less distracted from her work. Fida, the teacher who led the dyslexia support group, asked Harriet to find realistic ways to achieve this. 'What would you do if your friend talked to you? How would you avoid being distracted?'. Harriet eventually decided she would move away if she was being distracted by other students. Other students suggested she 'use the force' from Star Wars!

The students discussed self-blame and negative thinking at length and several of them, including Harriet, said they thought you should blame yourself and that they did blame themselves for not being good at their work. Fida suggested you could choose better ways to cope. She pointed out that Richard Branson, who has dyslexia, did not measure being 'smart' by his reading and writing. She suggested that being embarrassed or ashamed about such difficulties was not a clever way to cope. She said that it was okay to take responsibility and do something about it, but that blaming yourself just made you feel hopeless and unable to do anything.

Fida chose the balloon activity (see Session 5 'Activity' on page 39) to reinforce this message. Harriet wrote the words 'give up' on her balloon and jumped on it. She and the other students obviously enjoyed the activity and they enthusiastically shared the experience with the whole-class group. The father of one of the other students, a successful builder, who also had difficulties with reading and spelling, came to speak with the students about his experiences in school and how it felt not to be able to spell or read well. He explained how he had needed to refuse to accept his own and other people's negative expectations and thoughts to get where he was in life today.

Harriet reported to the group that she was having some success with her goal of not being distracted, but her class teacher, Steve, did not agree. Fida helped Harriet to use the problem-solving steps and they decided that the source of the problem was that Harriet was in fact still giving up and talking was her way of doing that. Together, Harriet and Fida generated ideas that might solve this problem. Finally, Harriet changed her goal to not giving up when she was asked to write in class. She decided instead to ask for help more often and to use the computer to help her with spelling words. Fida spoke with Steve about the change and Steve ensured he responded quickly when Harriet asked for help.

One day the group met in the gym, so Fida set up hurdles for the students to jump over. Harriet asked, 'What if I knock one over?'. Fida replied, 'Get up and try again. This course does not teach spelling but it does teach how to find different ways to manage difficult situations'.

Towards the end of the program Steve noted that:

> *Whereas at the beginning of the year Harriet was highlighting every single mistake and going 'oh that's a mistake and that's a mistake', now, she doesn't. She knows that she can type it into Microsoft Word and do a spell check on it. She still struggles but she'll at least recognise that she is struggling and just keep trying hard. Instead of just saying 'I can't do it, I'm stupid' or 'I'm dumb' or the things that she used to say, she will say to herself 'look I know I struggle at this but I'm going to try my best'. She's now recognising that she is doing something about it and she does ask for help a lot. And I think it was about making sure that she knew that it was okay to ask for help. She's improved her confidence a lot.*

Steve also related that he had heard Harriet stand up for herself in response to a boy telling her she was 'dumb'. She told the boy that she wasn't dumb but that she had difficulty with spelling. Harriet herself said she had learned from the program 'that if you think bad you feel bad'.

To finish the program the class made videos of how to cope with difficulties. Harriet and two of her friends made a video about not giving up when faced with a word that was difficult to spell. Instead they presented many options of how to respond when at first you don't succeed. These included asking a teacher, then asking a friend, and finally, despite the frustration of still not succeeding, going to the computer and using a spellchecker. Their final instruction to viewers was to never give up. Harriet's comment about the program was that it was 'hard but fun'.

Session 6

Choose powerful thoughts

Aims

- To show the connection between thoughts and feelings.
- To show how to think in a way that gives positive feelings and energy for positive action.

Session sequence

1. Revise coping strategy choices made last session.

> **REMINDERS**
>
> Personal goal progress:
> - During each session and at other opportunities take time to ask students to share progress with their personal goals.
> - It is important to give individual attention to each student and help him or her with ways to move towards their goal.
> - Success with a goal is a powerful way to convince students of the usefulness of the strategies in the program.
> - Praise all attempts even if they were not successful. Students need to know to reward and encourage themselves.
> - When one goal is fulfilled students can create a new goal.

2. Share with students the concept of powerful positive thinking (see the 'Key messages to share' below). Include a discussion of the meaning of 'positive' and 'negative' and generate a list of positive and negative feelings.
3. Discuss the 'Key messages' in the context of examples of difficult situations from either literature or students' own situations. Ask the class for examples of powerful, positive or put-down, negative self-talk responses.

Positive thinking and problem solving

KEY MESSAGES TO SHARE

Positive thinking

- Thoughts influence feelings.
- Positive thoughts increase positive feelings and give energy for powerful, positive action.
- Negative thoughts lead to feeling helpless, angry at yourself and other people, and feeling that the problem will never get better and that it affects all of your life.
- Positive thinkers are more successful at schoolwork, are healthier and have more friends.

Examples:

Positive, powerful thoughts

1. This test is harder than I expected but I will try my best and hopefully will get some of it right.
2. I can't remember how to spell this word. That is because I have learning disabilities. It does not mean I am stupid. I will ask Jenny to check my work before I hand it in.

Helpless negative thoughts

1. This test is too hard and I'll get it all wrong.
2. I can't remember how to spell this word. I must be really dumb. I'll give up on this assignment. It's too hard.

Activities

Cool Cat and Miserable Mouse

1. With the help of the class make a list on the whiteboard of difficult situations (see 'Examples' below).
2. In pairs or small groups use puppets or other props to create a Cool Cat (positive thinker) and Miserable Mouse (negative thinker) character.
3. Students choose a difficult situation for Cool Cat and Miserable Mouse to speak about. They ask each character how they feel and what they will do about the situation.

Listen to your self-talk

1. Ask students to relax, close or cover their eyes, and focus on their thoughts.
2. Describe a difficult situation and ask students to notice:
   - What they are saying to themselves. Is it positive (encouraging) or negative (discouraging)?
   - How do they feel?

> **EXAMPLES OF DIFFICULT SITUATIONS**
> - You are told you are messing around in class and must stay in at playtime.
> - You are writing a story and can't spell some words.
> - Your mother says you can't go out with your friends to a movie as she wants you to go with the family to see your aunt.

Thoughts on trial

1. Ask two students to present to the class 'true' and 'false' sides for a negative thought.
   - Example negative thought:

   She said she wouldn't come to my party. It means she doesn't like me. No one likes me much. I will never be popular. I wish I wasn't having the party at all.

2. Discuss the feelings and possible later action that may result from each response. Help the group to make a final helpful thought. Have the negative thinker say the 'new thought' and discuss any new feelings and possible actions she/he would take.

Partner coaches

1. Students work with a partner to think of two difficult situations related, if possible, to their personal goals. Students tell their self-talk to their partner.
2. Together they decide whether the self-talk is negative or positive and discuss whether it is accurate or not. Partners take turns to help each other choose positive self-talk.
3. Remind students to care for and encourage themselves and each other.

Helpful self-talk

- Provide colourful stickers on which there is room to write. Ask students to write a helpful self-talk message for each of their goals. Suggest they put it in a private place where they can frequently see it.

Positive thinking stories

- Create a cartoon or story, or act out a play to illustrate positive thinking. See also literature examples and activities in the *Gatehouse Project* (Centre for Adolescent Health, 2002, see Resources – General).

Positive help

▶ Students individually or as a group assist students in another class to think more positively.

Extension

▶ Extension activities for good readers/writers (see Resource lists for full details)
  ▷ *Coping for Success CD* by Erica Frydenberg
  ▷ *Gatehouse Project: Teaching Resources for Emotional Well-being* by the Centre for Adolescent Health.

Dyslexia support group

Link to Session 6

Aims

▶ To encourage students to relate the positive thinking strategies to dealing with situations that arise due to their dyslexia.

Session sequence

1. Discuss positive and negative thinking in relation to dyslexia.
2. Use the Session 6 'Activity' ideas with specific reference to students' dyslexia goals and situations.

EXAMPLE: THOUGHTS ON TRIAL

Scenario: You ask the student next to you how to spell a word. She says you are dumb for not knowing.

Feelings: Anger, hurt, embarrassment.

Thought: She's right. I am stupid.

Student 1	Student 2
Possible reasons self-talk may be true	**Possible reasons self-talk may be false**
I can't spell the word.	Maybe she can't spell it also but won't admit that.
	Maybe she is in a bad mood and is taking it out on me. The problem is hers, not mine.
	I am clever at many things. Not being able to spell a word does not make me stupid.

New thought: I had trouble spelling the word but I'm good at many other things. Not being good at spelling does not make me stupid. I am sure she is also not good at some things. I will not allow her to make me feel bad.

Feeling: OK.

Session 7

Problem solving

Aims

▶ To assist students to solve problems related to their personal goals.

Session sequence

1. Discuss students' progress with their goals:

   ▶ Remind students to use positive self-talk and effective coping strategies in relation to their goal.
   ▶ Use the problem-solving steps in the 'Key messages' to help students to progress with their personal goal.
   ▶ Assist students to choose another goal if they have achieved the original one or if they are unable to achieve it despite using the problem-solving steps.

> **KEY MESSAGES TO SHARE**
>
> Problem-solving steps:
> ▶ Say **exactly** what the problem is.
> ▶ Think of as many solutions as you can no matter how silly they seem. Ask other people for ideas.
> ▶ Decide which idea would work best.
> ▶ Make an **exact** plan of what you will do and when.
> ▶ Check in a short while how well your plan is working.
> ▶ Begin again at step one if you need to work further on your plan.
>
> Source: Adapted from Gordon, 1974.

Dyslexia support group

Link to Session 7

Aims

▶ *To assist students to deal with obstacles that prevent them from achieving their goals.*

Session sequence

1. *Use the problem-solving steps to help students with dyslexia-related problems achieve their personal goals.*
2. *Give individual attention to each student who has dyslexia to help him or her with ways to move towards their goal. Be ready to help students acknowledge their own efforts and progress (students who self-blame or are negative thinkers may discount their own efforts and progress).*

Part 3: Assertiveness and program finalisation

Sessions 8–11

Guidelines for teachers

Assertiveness (Sessions 8–10)

Assertiveness can be defined as the expression of one's rights and opinions while respecting those of others. While positive thinking helps to increase control of internal feelings, assertive communication takes this to the next step of working actively for positive change.

Assertiveness programs have been found to be effective in increasing one's sense of personal control and assertion skills, for adults as well as young people. The assertiveness section of this program aims to assist students in responding to their difficulties by working effectively to modify the situation, rather than directing anger at others, or withdrawing and ignoring their own needs. It is thus an active, productive coping strategy that involves focusing and working on the area of difficulty.

The component begins with developing awareness of the differences between assertion, aggression and passivity, and the likely consequences of using each type of response. Students then relate this knowledge to their own situations and practise using assertive body language and verbal responses.

Despite the many examples in films of successful outcomes from aggression, in real life aggressive people are not liked or regarded as successful. Aggression, while possibly giving short-term feelings of control, is associated with feelings of anger, guilt and fear. It involves standing up for oneself at the expense of the other person's needs and rights. It is an attack on the person rather than an objection to a particular situation or behaviour. Such aggression and bullying is associated with loss of friendship and it often leads to counter aggression. Students need to learn therefore that there are more effective ways than using aggression to deal with difficult situations.

Passivity or failing to defend oneself is also not an effective response. Such avoidance of confrontations may result in important needs not being met. Such responses may also be associated with indirect manipulation of others, depression, self-blame and a sense of worthlessness.

Assertiveness, by contrast, is likely to lead to successful outcomes as well as the self-respect and pride that comes from respecting both one's own and another person's needs. Assertiveness involves being open and direct about a difficult situation or behaviour without attacking or being disrespectful of the other person. Assertive people can stand up for themselves without offending others. They are viewed by other people as being reasonable, clear thinking and respectful. Constructing a specific, realistic request and then finding an appropriate time to deliver it in a calm manner is more likely to be successful than an angry, generalised complaint which lacks a way forward for the other person. Even if a desired outcome is not achieved, feeling assertively in control and respectfully standing up for oneself is a reward in itself.

This skill of assertiveness takes time to develop. Repeated opportunities to practise, both in class role plays and in real life, will assist students to learn to use it. Modelling by teachers and other adults will also help students to see that it is a response that works well. Students are likely to also need explicit teaching that assertiveness involves pre-planning. It includes taking time to recognise difficult feelings such as anger and sadness, to think through what it is that is really wanted and working out how best to achieve that.

Body language is also an important component of assertiveness. Posture, gestures, eye contact, voice tone, physical distance and facial expression all convey more than the actual words spoken. Students need opportunities to practise taking control of their body language so that they can convey the messages they intend to convey.

Learning to be assertive also includes learning to use perseverance and flexibility in the face of refusals, listening to and taking account of the other person's feelings and needs, refusing to get caught in anger spirals, learning to compromise and taking the lead by suggesting solutions. While students may not master all the complexities involved it is important to introduce them to these aspects of assertiveness. This can best be done during discussion within the program sessions and also by discussing with individual students their progress with using assertive skills in their own real-life situations, particularly in the context of achieving their chosen goals.

Revision and finalisation (Session 11)

This final section of the program is an opportunity to revise the skills and strategies presented, to reflect on progress made in integrating these as default responses to challenges presented by difficult situations, and to finalise and celebrate completion of the program. The various activities presented in this section achieve these aims.

It is important to ensure that each student has an opportunity to discuss and reflect on progress regarding completion of their goal. If students have not succeeded in achieving their goal it will be important that they have a chance to have closure on this. They may decide to work towards another goal or to come to understand why they did not achieve the goal they set and how they could modify it so that it is achievable.

Celebrating completion of the program will reflect its importance and help students to acknowledge their own efforts and to feel positive about their experience of the program and the skills involved. Finally, it will be important to continue to reinforce the program skills and strategies on a regular basis within the classroom following the completion of the actual program.

Jake's story

Jake was a shy boy in Grade 6 who had been diagnosed with a significant learning difficulty. His school report noted that he needed to concentrate more in class and seek help more often, and that he had not handed in all his work. His teacher recounted that Jake would often tell the teacher he understood, when in fact he didn't, that he was withdrawn and 'closed' and had a hopeless image of himself with regard to his learning difficulties. In class, Jake often sat in a hunched or floppy position with his face lowered and blank and took little or no part in class discussion. If he did speak it was in a soft voice and his parents and teachers felt that he had trouble standing up for himself.

Jake took part in the dyslexia support group. Initially, in this smaller group situation, Jake quietly answered questions but he gave little eye contact. This small group spent several sessions practising the assertive response role plays. They chose difficult situations from their own lives to work on in the role plays. Often the situations related to their chosen goals for the program.

Jake's role play addressed his conflict with his younger brother whom he saw as being protected by his parents and as always getting his own way. At first Jake used aggression or withdrawal in the role play. He was also passive in response to a student developed role play of being called 'dumb' by another student. He said afterwards he felt he should have known how to stand up to this but didn't know what to say.

By the third session, however, Jake defended another student whom he felt was a victim of teacher misunderstanding. The Bill of Rights (see *Handout 7* on page 67) had been discussed during the previous session. Jake encouraged a fellow student by saying with conviction, 'You have rights. You can't lose all your life'. After this session, Jake began arriving to the sessions smiling and looking relaxed. By the time his role play was videoed he repeated a well thought out, reasonable request in a calm, firm voice and used sustained eye contact. During this last session, the teacher asked the group what they felt about the program. Jake responded that he did not feel shy to put up his hand in class now.

By the end of the program Jake had become more assertive and more engaged in class. It was observed in the classroom, at the end of the program, that Jake called out to the teacher quite loudly that he had some completed homework with him. He looked alert and sat up straight at his desk, initiated borrowing a work sheet, talked to the girls at the next desk and received a note from them, and put his hand up and asked a question in front of the class. Jake's class teacher commented that he asked more questions, had a more upright, confident posture, and was more persistent about getting his needs met: 'He's probably a bit more persistent too, in that, if he doesn't understand it the first time he'll ask again, which is really good'. She added that Jake was asking her for information he had missed, and that he 'sticks to his guns, even if he is not sure'. Jake's parents felt he had become more direct, more persistent in pursuing what he wanted, less sensitive, more articulate, confident and relaxed. His mother said he is 'probably more up-front now, whereas before he'd probably beat around the bush a little bit more'.

Jake himself commented about the program that he had found out:

Not to always sit back and do what other people want you to do. You can have a say in that, and you go ahead and do what you want to do. You can stand up for yourself rather than feeling sad.

Jake's father felt his academic work had improved and that he had become more articulate, open and confident. He said:

He's changed. He thinks he can read and everything now. His vocabulary is a lot better. He can explain himself pretty well. He was more withdrawn before, whereas he's more chatty now. He's more at ease [with] the way he handles every situation. The tension isn't there anymore. The anger is gone. The anger was from [thinking] he was dumb. His voice is more assertive now because he knows he's confident in what he is saying, that's the difference. His approach is more upright and forthright. When you have the confidence you're going to stand up proud.

The dyslexia support group teacher said Jake was:

A boy who was no longer ashamed of his learning problem, who was no longer worried he did not have power and control over his world. He could communicate with his fellow students and not feel they were judging him by his learning difficulties. He is a young man who I believe has a positive attitude to school, and who believes that whatever he wants he will be able to get somehow.

Session 8

Why be assertive?

Aims

▶ To explore and practise assertive, verbal and non-verbal communication.

> **KEY MESSAGES TO SHARE**
>
> What is assertiveness?
> ▶ *Assertiveness* is standing up for yourself and solving your own problems without hurting other people. It is being in control of yourself, taking account of your needs and the other person's needs.
> ▶ *Aggressiveness* is trying to get what you want by attacking someone. It often shows you have lost control of yourself. The other person's needs are not taken into account.
> ▶ *Passiveness* is not standing up for yourself when someone hurts you. It is not taking control of the situation and your needs are not taken into account.

Session sequence

1. Discuss the difference between assertion, aggression and passivity and the advantages of being assertive (see 'Key messages to share', and 'Examples of aggression, passivity and assertion' below, as well as *Handout 3: Can you keep your balance?*).
2. Discuss the feelings and probable consequences that accompany aggression, passivity and assertion and ask for student responses about why each kind of behaviour is used (see *Handout 4: Reasons, feelings and consequences for assertion, aggression and passivity*).
3. Discuss students' own situations and the consequences of responding assertively, aggressively or passively. These questions may guide discussion:
   ▶ What was the situation?
   ▶ How did you respond?

- Was the action assertive, aggressive or passive?
- Why did you respond that way?
- How did you feel?
- Was the outcome what you wanted?

Activities

- Ask students to complete simple activities (e.g. walk around the room, sit in a chair) aggressively, passively and assertively. Change the style at a given signal, for example, a designated student rings a bell.
- Integrate the assertion balance concept (see *Handout 3: Can you keep your balance?*) with maths weights and measures or physical education balance activities.
- Ask student volunteers to role play the three different styles: aggressive, passive and assertive (see *Handout 5: Scenario examples for assertion practice*). Emphasise the differences and the advantages of using assertion. Encourage discussion of how in control students feel and the probable consequences for each style.
- Draw a symbol for each style and make up a nickname for it. Associate each style with feelings (see *Handout 6: Assertive, aggressive or passive?* Examples of nicknames are: aggro/aggressive, wimp/passive, owl/assertive).
- Look at excerpts from TV shows (or from literature) for assertive, aggressive or passive behaviour. The following questions may guide discussion:
  - What was the situation?
  - How did the person respond?
  - Was the action assertive, aggressive or passive?
  - Why did they respond that way?
  - How did they feel?
  - Was the outcome what they wanted?
- Discuss the rights students believe they have. Include United Nations' support for Children's Rights (see *Handout 7: My Bill of Rights*). Point out that each person also has the right to choose when or whether to assert his or her rights, and there may be times when they decide it is best not to do so.
- In a relaxation session run a body sweep for feelings. Use the 'feelings colour key' from *Handout 6*. Students colour in on the body chart (see *Handout 8: How do you feel?*) the feelings they discovered in their bodies. Point out that feelings of anger, sadness or depression may indicate a need for making a plan for assertive action. Discuss helpful ways of dealing with difficult feelings.

EXAMPLES OF AGGRESSION, PASSIVITY AND ASSERTION

Joining a group

Passive: Standing near the group, saying nothing, not looking at people, slumped body, no smile.

Aggressive: Advancing quickly, hands on hips, interrupting in a loud voice.

Assertive: Standing upright and smiling, listening, looking interested, using a calm voice to ask to join in.

Not being able to do some work in class

Passive: Doing nothing, not asking for help, slumping over the desk and looking miserable.

Aggressive: Scribbling over the work, hitting someone, yelling at your friend or at the teacher.

Assertive: Going up to the teacher using a firm voice to tell the teacher what is hard about the work, asking the teacher for what you need to make the work easier (e.g. help to read the assignment), keeping on trying to get the teacher's help even if the teacher is busy.

You ask a classmate how to spell a word. She says you are dumb for not knowing.

Passive: You say nothing and believe what is said about you. You feel miserable.

Aggressive: You hit at her and yell, 'What do you know, Fatso?'

Assertive: Look the classmate in the eyes and say calmly and clearly, 'I am not dumb. I am clever at many things, but I can't spell some words.'

Handout 3: Can you keep your balance?

Balancing your needs and others' needs makes a difference.

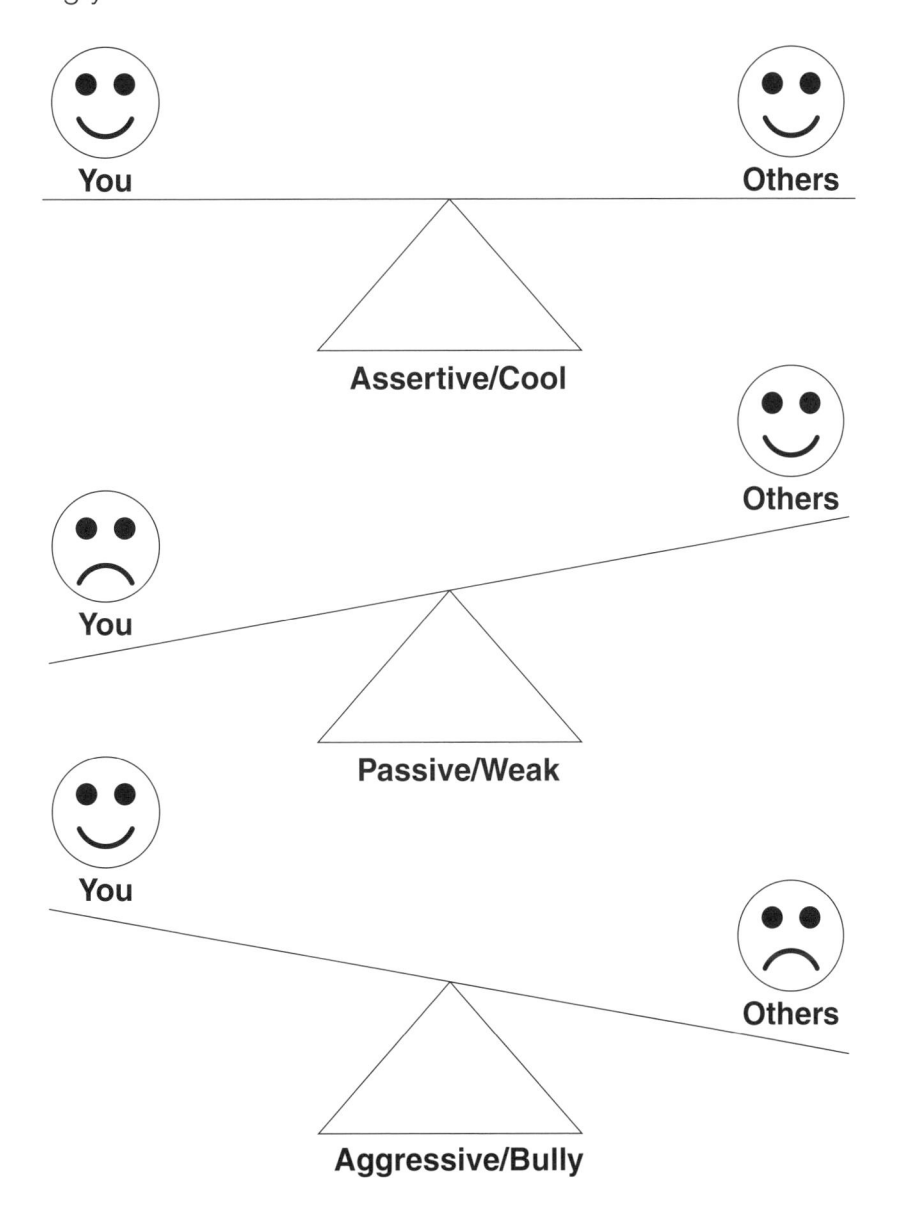

Assertive/Cool

Passive/Weak

Aggressive/Bully

Success and Dyslexia © Nola Firth and Erica Frydenberg 2011

Handout 4: Reasons, feelings and consequences for assertion, aggression and passivity

	Reasons	**Feelings**	**Consequences**
Passivity	▶ Being afraid of standing up to the other person ▶ Being used to letting other people protect you	▶ Depression ▶ Sadness ▶ Worthlessness	▶ Not getting what you need
Aggression	▶ Not knowing what else to do ▶ Short-term feeling of being powerful	▶ Anger ▶ Guilt ▶ Fear	▶ Aggressive response ▶ Loss of friendship *(Research shows that bullies are not successful or liked.)*
Assertion	▶ Knowing how to be assertive ▶ Wanting to stay in control ▶ Wanting to include the needs of others	▶ Pride ▶ Self-respect ▶ Happiness	▶ Both people feeling respected ▶ Your needs accepted

Source: Adapted from Firth, 2001a

Success and Dyslexia © Nola Firth and Erica Frydenberg 2011

Handout 5: Scenario examples for assertion practice

- Your teacher is angry with you in class because you are not working. Many others in the class are working but it looks difficult to you.

- Your mum blames you for making your younger brother angry, but actually he switched the TV channel without asking you so you turned it back to the original channel. Your brother then told your mum you were annoying him.

- Your new teacher tells you your work is untidy, but you always have trouble making your writing look neat.

- Your friend Jim wants to borrow your bike for the weekend and you are not allowed to lend it to him.

Source: Adapted from Firth, 2001a

Success and Dyslexia

Handout 6: Assertive, aggressive or passive?

▶ Draw a symbol for each kind of behaviour and make up a nickname for it.
▶ Colour code the feelings key, then colour in the symbols with the colour that matches the feeling.

Aggressive/_____

Passive/_____

Assertive/_____

Feelings colour key:

Feeling	Colour
Sad	
Happy	
Worried	
Angry	
Proud	
Afraid	
Confident	

Success and Dyslexia © Nola Firth and Erica Frydenberg 2011

Handout 7: My Bill of Rights

(These rights are taken from the United Nations Convention on the Rights of the Child adopted in 1989 by the General Assembly of the United Nations, and ratified by Australia in 1990.)

☐ I have the right to be treated with respect as an equal human being.

☐ I have the right to express my feelings and opinions.

☐ I have the right to say yes and no for myself (even to an adult, if the request will cause me harm or is illegal).

☐ I have the right to make mistakes.

☐ I have the right to change my mind.

☐ I have the right to ask for what I want.

☐ I have the right to not take on responsibility for other people's problems.

☐ I have the right to _____

_____

_____

1. Tick the rights you accept as being fair.

2. The blank section above is a place to add any rights you feel should also be there.

Success and Dyslexia

Handout 8: How do you feel?

Use the feelings goal key on *Handout 6: Assertive, aggressive or passive?* to colour in what you feel and where in your body you feel it.

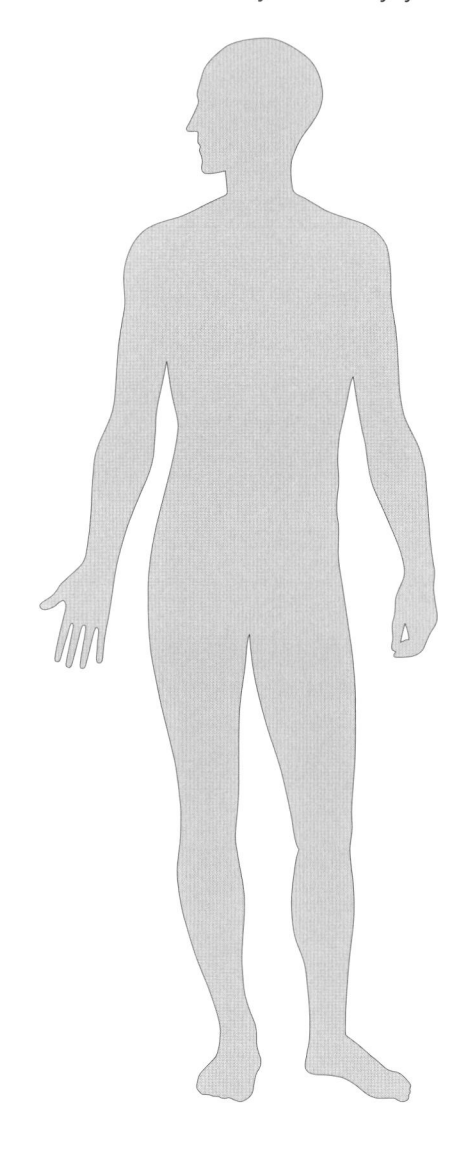

Success and Dyslexia © Nola Firth and Erica Frydenberg 2011

Session 9

Assertive language

Aims

▶ To explore and practise using assertive language.

Session sequence

1. Revise coping choices, positive thinking and assertiveness.
2. Discuss students' progress with their goals.
3. Teach the parts of an assertive request and tips for making the request (see 'Key messages' below).
4. Ask students to make up an assertive request that would help with a situation (preferably in relation to their personal goal) where they have a problem with what someone else is doing (see *Handout 9: Say what you want*).

> **KEY MESSAGES TO SHARE**
>
> **Assertive messages**
> ▶ Begin with 'I....' followed by how you feel (e.g. I feel upset...).
> ▶ Say exactly what makes you feel that way (e.g. that I am not allowed to go out with my friends).
> ▶ Say why you feel that way (e.g. because it makes me feel left out).
> ▶ Say what you want instead (e.g. I would like to go out with my friends next Saturday night).
>
> *Example of an assertive request:*
> *When I'm watching TV, I feel upset when you change the channel. I would like you to ask me first.*
>
> Tips on being assertive
> ▶ Be ready to keep saying your request. It is likely to be resisted at first.
> ▶ Feel your feelings before you say your assertive request. This helps you to stay calm even if the other person gets angry.
> ▶ Don't get caught up in anger spirals. Listen calmly, say you can see the other person feels angry, and then calmly and politely repeat your request.
> ▶ Take the other person's needs into account. Suggesting a compromise may be a good solution.

Activities

- Students prepare assertive requests and practise saying them to a partner. The partner gives feedback on whether the request is assertive (spoken in the first person, use of blame-free language, specific rather than general request, and calm, confident expression of voice). Students then say the request three times to their partner using passive, aggressive and assertive body language. The partner has to guess the order used. (Note: It is not necessary to keep to the exact language of the assertive request. The most important part is that students take the initiative to work out and ask clearly, calmly and specifically for what they want.)
- In small groups create a cartoon, story or role-play script where angry responses and other distractions are listened to, but the assertive message is repeated calmly.
- Invite a conflict resolution expert to speak to the class or discuss international diplomacy and conflict resolution.

Handout 9: Say what you want

Fill in the assertive way of asking for what you want.

Assertive Statement 1

When _____

I feel _____

I would like _____

Assertive Statement 2

When _____

I feel _____

I would like _____

Assertive Statement 3

When _____

I feel _____

I would like _____

Success and Dyslexia © Nola Firth and Erica Frydenberg 2011

Session 10

Assertive body messages

Aims

▶ To explore and practise assertive body messages.

Session sequence

1. Revise coping choices, positive thinking and assertiveness.
2. Discuss with students how they are progressing with their goals.
3. Tell students that we know people take more notice of body messages than words. Discuss, model and ask students to assume aggressive, assertive and passive body positions.

> **EXAMPLE OF ASSERTIVE, PASSIVE AND AGGRESSIVE BODY LANGUAGE**
>
> **Aggression:** *Hands on hips, looking down nose, eyes open wide, loud voice, moving in close.*
> **Passivity:** *No eye contact, slouching, head on one side, soft voice, giggling.*
> **Assertion:** *Calm, firm voice, appropriate physical distance.*

Activities

▶ Students walk around the room until the teacher calls a 'freeze' body position as assertive, aggressive or passive.
▶ Students form pairs and take it in turns to ask for an object (e.g. a pen). The requester must use an assertive body position and voice before they receive the object. At the end of the activity, students discuss their own and their partner's body language.
▶ Students form pairs and take it in turns to role play, assertively asking for something they want in relation to their personal goal. The partner gives helpful feedback. Students could

present the role play for the whole group and/or video it (see 'Role-play methodology' below).
- As homework ask students to try using assertiveness skills with friends or family. Be sure to discuss the outcome.
- See also assertion activities in *Stop Think Do: Teachers' Manual for Training Social Skills while Managing Student Behaviour* (Peterson & Gannoni, 1989, see Resources – General), and the *Gatehouse Project* (Centre for Adolescent Health, 2002, pp 90–91, see Resources – General).

Role-play methodology

1. A student chooses a scenario in which they want to practise being more assertive. They then choose a partner to role play with them and tell that person where the scene is taking place, the appearance, character and behaviour of the person they are pretending to be.
2. The students set up the scene using available props and play the scene for the group.
3. Freeze the play after about two minutes to check with the original student as to: the match with the real situation, how he/she is feeling, whether he/she feels in control, whether their current response worked and what changes they would like.
4. Re-run or continue the role play.
5. Refreeze and repeat step 3 above. Also ask for feedback from the group on assertiveness of the student's words and body language and take other suggestions. Reassure the student that they only need to take on feedback from the group if it feels useful.
6. Finish the role play when positive change begins to occur.
7. The following variations can also be useful: role reversal, other students doing the role play while the original student who designed the scenario watches, inclusion of another student saying probable feelings of the players, and playing the desired scene rather than the present difficult one.
8. Allow time for final discussion, remembering to include the student who set up the role play as well as encouraging feedback from other group members.
9. Ask the original student to sum up what they have learned.

Dyslexia support group

Link to Sessions 8–10

Aims

- *To relate assertion skills to coping with dyslexia.*
- *To give intensive practice at using assertion strategies within a supportive environment.*
- *To give students opportunities to learn to self-advocate in regard to their dyslexia.*

Session sequence

1. *Practise assertive requests that relate to situations students face with regard to having dyslexia (see 'Example' below).*
2. *Use the small group situation to act out role plays to help students practise their assertive requests (see* Handout 9: Say what you want*). Examples of assertive requests that may be relevant for students who have dyslexia include:*
   - *asking for help with work*
   - *explaining what they don't understand and why*
   - *asking for extensions for assignments*
   - *asking for use of print-free presentation of projects, for example, an oral presentation*
   - *asking for repetition of information*
   - *asking for access to speech-to-print software or to electronic, non-print sources of information*
   - *asking for opportunities to be involved in areas in which they have strengths.*

Activities

- *Video the role plays once students have practised them and are confident.*
- *Have students make DVDs of mini-plays about how to deal with difficulties, such as not being able to spell a word.*

▶ *Have students run their own Individual Education Plan (IEP) meeting. They might design and send invitations, learn to chair the meeting and tell the group their strengths and difficulties, how they best learn and what they would like.*

> **EXAMPLE OF AN ASSERTIVE DYSLEXIA REQUEST**
>
> ▶ When you ask me to read out loud in front of the class, I am embarrassed. I would like not to have to do that in public.

Session 11

Revision and finalisation

Aims

- To revise and integrate the program strategies.
- To finalise the program.

Activities

- Run an oral quiz based on the course content to this point. Small rewards for correct answers may increase enjoyment of the activity.
- Questions may include the following:
  - What is definitely an unhelpful coping strategy that some people use?
  - What are four helpful coping strategies?
  - What does an assertive person's face and body look like?
  - What are two assertive strategies you can use?
  - What is self-talk?
  - How do you make self-talk positive?
  - Why is it important to use positive self-talk?
  - What is an area of your life where you can always take control no matter what is happening for you?
  - What is the difference between assertion and aggression?
  - What is the difference between assertion and passivity?
- Re-run the *Adolescent Coping Scale 2nd edition* or the 'How Do You Cope Profile'. Compare these with those completed at the beginning of the program. Discuss how students feel about any changes that have occurred in how they cope with challenges.
- In groups, ask the students to prepare a PowerPoint presentation or other activity that teaches Grade 5 students about clever coping, positive thinking and assertion. They choose one to present to the Grade 5s.
- Make a snakes and ladders game using coping strategies, positive and negative thinking and assertion, aggression and passivity. Students pair with a younger child and use the game to help teach clever coping to their partner.
- Make a poster advertising positive thinking, clever coping or assertion.

- Talk with each student about his or her personal goal and strategy progress. Modification of the goal may be needed if there is lack of progress. If the goal was achieved, celebrate this. New goals may also be made.
- Distribute *Success and Dyslexia* completion certificates (see page 78) in the context of a final party.

CONGRATULATIONS

THIS IS TO CERTIFY THAT

HAS SUCCESSFULLY PARTICIPATED IN

Success and Dyslexia.

Well Done!

Success and Dyslexia © Nola Firth and Erica Frydenberg 2011

Bibliography

Bryan, T., Burstein, K., & Ergul, C. (2004). The social-emotional side of learning disabilities: A science-based presentation of the state of the art. *Learning Disabilities Quarterly, 27*(1), 45–51.

Chan, L., & Dally, K. (2000). Review of literature. In W. Louden, L. Chan, J. Elkins, D. Greaves, H. House, M. Milton, S. Nichols, M. Rohl, J. Rivalland, & C. Van Kraayenoord (Eds.), *Mapping the territory: Primary students with learning difficulties: Literacy and numeracy* (Vol. 2, pp. 161–331). Canberra: Department of Education, Training and Youth Affairs.

Deshler, D. (2005). Adolescents with learning disabilities: Unique challenges and reasons for hope. *Learning Disability Quarterly, 28*, 122–125.

Dweck, C. (2000). *Self theories: Their role in motivation, personality, and development*. Philadelphia: Psychology Press.

Dyslexia working party. (2010). *Helping people with dyslexia: A national agenda*. Report to Hon. Bill Shorten, Parliamentary Secretary for Disabilities and Children's Services. Retrieved 23 March, 2010 from http://www.ldaustralia.org/dyslexia_action_agenda_1.doc

Fensham, P., Gunstone, R., & White, R. (1994). *The content of science*. London: The Falmer Press.

Firth, N. (2001a). *Taking charge*. Melbourne: Ozchild.

Firth, N. (2001b). *Taking charge: A pilot study of the effect of an assertiveness program on assertiveness and locus of control orientation of young adolescents with specific learning difficulties* (Unpublished master's thesis). The University of Melbourne, Melbourne, Australia.

Firth, N. (2009). How do adolescents cope with learning disabilities? *Australian Journal of Dyslexia and Learning Difficulties, 4*, 23–29.

Firth, N., Butler, H., Drew, S., Krelle, A., Sheffield, J., Patton, G., Tollit, M., Bond, L., & the beyondblue project management team (2008). Implementing multi-level programs and approaches that address student wellbeing and connectedness: Factoring in the needs of the schools. *Advances in School Mental Health Promotion 1*(4), 14–24.

Frydenberg, E. (2008). *Adolescent coping: Advances in theory, research and practice*. London: Routledge.

Frydenberg, E., & Brandon, C. (2007). *The best of coping*. Melbourne: ACER Press.

Frydenberg, E., & Lewis, R. (2011). *Adolescent coping scale* (2nd ed.). Melbourne: ACER Press.

Frydenberg, E., Lewis, R., Bugalski, K., Cotta, A., McCarthy, C., Luscombe-Smith, N., Poole, C. (2004). Prevention is better than cure: Coping skills training for adolescents at school. *Educational Psychology in Practice, 20*(2), 119–134.

Bibliography

Goldberg, R. J., Higgins, E. L., Raskind, M. H., & Herman, K. L. (2003). Predictors of success in individuals with learning disabilities: A qualitative analysis of a 20-year longitudinal study. *Learning Disabilities Research and Practice, 4*, 222–236.

Gresham, F. (1998). Social skills training: Should we raze, remodel, or rebuild? *Behavioral Disorders, 24*(1), 19–25.

Lackaye, T., Margalit, M., Ziv, O., & Ziman, T. (2006). Comparisons of self-efficacy, mood, effort, and hope between students with learning disabilities and their non-LD-matched peers. *Learning Disabilities Research & Practice, 21*(2), 111–121.

Louden, W., Chan, L., Elkins, J., Greaves, D., House, H., Milton, M., Nichols, S., Rohl, M., Rivalland, J., & Van Krayenoord, C. (2000). *Mapping the territory, primary students with learning difficulties: Literacy and numeracy.* Canberra: Department of Education, Training and Youth Affairs.

Margalit, M. (2003). Resilience model among individuals with learning disabilities: Proximal and distal influences. *Learning Disabilities Research and Practice, 18*(2), 82–86.

Nalavany, B. A., Carawan, L. W., & Renick, R. A. (2011). Psychosocial experiences associated with confirmed and self identified dyslexia: A participant-driven concept map of adult perspectives. *Journal of Learning Disabilities, 44*, 63–79.

National Health and Medical Research Council. (1990). *Learning difficulties in children and adolescents.* Canberra: Australian Government Publishing Service.

Núñez, C. J., Gonzalez-Pienda, J. A., Gonzalez-Pumariega, S., Roces, C., Alvarez, L., & Gonzalez, P. (2005). Subgroups of attributional profiles in students with learning difficulties and their relation to self-concept and academic goals. *Learning Disabilities Research and Practice, 20*(2), 86–97.

Perez, M., & Reicharts, M. (1992). *Stress, coping and health.* Seattle: Hogrefe and Huber.

Prior, M. (1996). *Understanding specific learning difficulties.* Hove, UK: Psychology Press.

Purdie, N., & Ellis, L. (2005). *Literature review: A review of the empirical evidence identifying effective interventions and teaching practices for students with learning difficulties in years 4,5, and 6.* Melbourne: Australian Council for Educational Research.

Raskind, M. H., Golberg, R. J., Higgins, E. L., & Herman, K. L. (1999). Patterns of change and predictors of success in individuals with learning disabilities: Results from a twenty-year study. *Learning Disabilities Research and Practice, 14*(1), 35–49.

Raskind, M. H., Golberg, R. J., Higgins, E. L., & Herman, K. L. (2002). Teaching 'life success' to students with LD: Lessons learned from a 20-year study. *Intervention in school and clinic, 37*(4), 201–208.

Reiff, H.B., Ginsberg, R., and Gerber, P. J. (1995). New perspectives on teaching from successful adults with learning disabilities. *Remedial and Special Education, 16*(1), 29–37.

Rodis, P., Garrod, A., &. Boscardin, M. L. (2001). *Learning disabilities and life stories.* Needham Heights, MA: Allyn & Bacon.

Rose, J. (2009) *Identifying and teaching children and young people with dyslexia and literacy difficulties.* London: Department of Children, Schools and Families.

Scanlon, D., & Mellard, D. (2002). Academic and participation profiles of school age dropouts with and without disabilities. *Exceptional Children, 68*(2), 239–258.

Shapiro, D.H. Jr., & Astin, J.A. (1998). *Control therapy: An integrated approach to psychotherapy, health, and healing.* New York: John Wiley and Sons.

Shaywitz, S. E., Morris, R., & Shaywitz, B. A. (2008). The education of dyslexic children from childhood to young adulthood. *Annual Review of Psychology, 59,* 451–475.

Sideris, G. D. (2007). Why are LD students depressed? A goal orientation model of depression vulnerability. *Journal of Learning Disabilities, 40*(6), 526–539.

Svetaz, M. V., Ireland, M., & Blum, R. (2000). Adolescents with learning disabilities: Risk and protective factors associated with emotional well-being: Findings from the National Longitudinal Study of Adolescent Health. *Journal of Adolescent Health, 27,* 340–348.

UNICEF. (n.d.) *Convention on the rights of the child.* Fact sheets – Rights under the Convention on the Rights of the Child. Retrieved 3 August, 2011 from www.unicef.org/crc/index_30228.html

Wechsler, D. (2003). *Wechsler intelligence scale for children* (4th ed.). San Antonio, TX: PsychCorp.

Wehmeyer, M. L., & Kelchner, K. (1995). *The Arc's self-determination scale.* Arlington, TX: The Arc.

Westwood, P. (2001). Differentiation as a strategy for inclusive classroom practice: Some difficulties identified. *Australian Journal of Learning Disabilities*, 6(1), 5–11.

Resources – General

Publications

Bourgeois, P., & Clark, B. (1986) *Franklin in the Dark*. Gosford, New South Wales: Ashton Scholastic.

Brandon, C. M., & Cunningham, E. G. (1999). *Bright ideas*. Melbourne: Ozchild.

Centre for Adolescent Health. (2002). *Gatehouse project: Teaching resources for emotional well-being*. Parkville, Victoria: Centre for Adolescent Health.

Field, E. M. (1999). *Bullybusting: How to help children deal with teasing and bullying*. Sydney: Finch Publishing.

Frydenberg, E. (2007). *Coping for success: Skills for everyday living* [CD]. Melbourne: University of Melbourne and ACER Press.

Frydenberg, E. (2010). *Think positively: A course for developing coping skills in adolescents*. London: Continuum.

Frydenberg, E., & Brandon, C. (2007). *The best of coping*. Melbourne: ACER Press.

Frydenberg, E., & Lewis, R. (2011). *Adolescent coping scale* (2nd ed.). Melbourne: ACER Press.

Gordon, T. (1974). *Teacher effectiveness training*. New York: David McKay Co.

McGrath, H., & Francey, S. (1991). *Friendly kids, friendly classrooms: Teaching social skills and confidence in the classroom*. Melbourne: Longman Cheshire.

Morris, E. (2004). *Assertiveness for middle school students*. Melbourne: ACER Press.

National Mental Health in Schools Project. (2000). *Mind matters: A mental health promotion resource for secondary schools*. Canberra: Commonwealth Department of Health and Aged Care.

Peterson, L., & Gannoni, A.F. (1989). *Stop think do: Teachers' manual for training social skills while managing student behaviour*. St. Mary's, South Australia: Stop Think Do Pty. Ltd.

Rickards, Jenny. (1994). *Relaxation for children*. Melbourne: ACER Press.

Seligman, M. (1995). *The optimistic child*. Sydney: Random House.

Seuss, Dr. (1967). *I had trouble getting to Solla Sollew*. New York: Random House.

Seuss, Dr. (1990). *Oh the places you'll go*. New York: Random House.

Useful websites

Authentic Happiness
www.authentichappiness.org
Martin Seligman's reflective happiness site includes online assessments (e.g. strengths).

CASEL (Collaborative for academic and social emotional learning)
http://casel.org/
This website has many resources including school climate assessments.

Gatehouse Project
http://wellbeingaustralia.com.au/Gatehouse%20project%20resources.pdf
This site contains teaching resources for emotional well-being, with downloadable materials available.

Mindmatters
http://www.mindmatters.edu.au/default.asp
Mindmatters is a mental health promotion support program for secondary schools. Downloadable materials are also available.

Resources – Dyslexia

Publications

Andrew, M. (1994). *Reading and spelling made simple*. Melbourne: ACER Press.

Branson, R. (2006). *Screw it, let's do it*. Milson's Point, New South Wales: Random House Australia.

Brent, M., Gough, F., & Robinson, S. (2001). *One in eleven*. Melbourne: ACER Press.

Byers, S., & Outrim, D. (2001). *Reading made easy: How to teach students experiencing difficulties with learning*. Perth: B+G Resource Enterprises.

Channel 4 & Poseidon Films (Producers). (1993). *Dyslexia – An avoidable national tragedy* [video]. Available from Hope Line Videos: http://www.hopelinevideos.com

Coil, C. (1994). *Motivating underachievers: 172 strategies for success*. Melbourne: Hawker Brownlow Education.

Firth, N., Frydenberg, E., & Greaves, D. (2006). Shared needs: Teachers helping students with learning disabilities to cope more effectively. In R. Lambert & C. McCarthy (Eds.), *Understanding stress in an age of accountability* (pp 65–86). Greenwich, CT: Information Age Publishing.

Frank, R., & Livingston, K. (2002). *The secret life of the dyslexic child: A practical guide for parents and educators*. Basingstoke, UK: Rodale Ltd.

Frostig Center. (2009). *The six success factors for children with learning disabilities: Ready-to-use activities to help kids with LD succeed in school and in life*. San Francisco, CA: Jossey-Bass.

Giangreco, M. F. (2002). *Quick-guides to inclusion 3: Ideas for educating students with disabilities*. London: Paul Brookes Publishing Co.

Lavoie, R. (1989). *How difficult can this be?: Understanding learning disabilities* [video]. Alexandria: PBS Video.

Louden, W., Chan, L., Elkins, J., Greaves, D., House, H., Milton, M., Nichols, S., Rohl, M., Rivalland, J., & Van Krayenoord, C. (2000). *Mapping the territory – Primary students with learning difficulties: Literacy and numeracy*. Retrieved from http://www.dest.gov.au/sectors/school_education/publications_resources/profiles/mapping_territory_primary_students_difficulties.htm

McGrath, H., & Noble, T. (1993). *Different kids, same classroom*. Melbourne: Longman Cheshire.

Prior, M. (1996). *Understanding specific learning difficulties*. Hove UK: Psychology Press.

Raskind, M. H., Golberg, R. J., Higgins, E. L., & Herman, K. L. (2002). Teaching 'life success' to students with LD: Lessons learned from a 20-year study. *Intervention in school and clinic, 37*(4), 201–208.

Raskind, M. H., Golberg, R. J., Higgins, E. L., & Herman, K. L. (2003). *Life success for children with learning disabilities: A parent guide*. Pasadena, CA: Frostig Centre. Download available from http://www.ldsuccess.org/pdf/LifeSuccessParentGuide.pdf

Reiff, H. B., Ginsberg, R., & Gerber, P. J. (1995). New perspectives on teaching from successful adults with learning disabilities. *Remedial and Special Education, 16*(1), 29–37.

Rodis, P., Garrod, A., &. Boscardin, M. L. (2001). *Learning disabilities and life stories*. Needham Heights, MA: Allyn & Bacon.

Smith, B. (1990). *Success stories in spite of early learning problems* [book and video]. East Brisbane, Queensland: Betty Smith.

Sydenham, S., & Thomas, R. (2001). *Acquiring research skills: Book 3*. Oxford, UK: Oxford University Press.

TVNZ. (2007). *Decoding dyslexia* [DVD]. Auckland, New Zealand: Author. Available from http://tvnz.co.nz/content/992327/2661645.html

Vaughn, S., Gersten, R., & Chard, D. (2000). The underlying message in LD intervention research: Findings from research syntheses. *Exceptional Children, 67*(1), 99–114.

Westwood, P. (1997). *Commonsense methods for children with special needs*. London: Routledge.

Westwood, P. (2006). *Teaching and learning difficulties*. Melbourne: ACER Press.

Winebrenner, S. (1996). *Teaching kids with learning difficulties in the regular classroom: Strategies and techniques every teacher can use to challenge and motivate struggling students*. Minneapolis, MN: Free Spirit Publishing.

Winkler, H., & Oliver, L. (2003). *I got a D in salami*. New York: Grosset and Dunlap.

Reports

Dyslexia working party. (2010). *Helping people with dyslexia: A national agenda*. Report to Hon. Bill Shorten, Parliamentary Secretary for Disabilities and Children's Services. Available from http://www.ldaustralia.org/dyslexia_action_agenda_1.doc

Firth, N. (2010). *To assess resilience programs for children who have specific learning disabilities*. Report to the Winston Churchill Memorial Trust of Australia. Available from http://www.churchilltrust.com.au/site_media/fellows/FIRTH_Nola_2009.pdf

This report is an investigation of resilience programs and environments for students who have specific learning disabilities/dyslexia in the US, UK and Canada.

Community websites

The Australian Federation of Specific Learning Difficulties Associations (AUSPELD)
http://www.auspeld.org.au/
AUSPELD is a non-political, non-sectarian association of parents and professional people interested in providing resources to assist children and adults with specific learning difficulties. There are branches in each state of Australia.

Resources – Dyslexia

Australian Learning Disabilities Association
> http://www.adcet.edu.au/alda/

This is the site for the Australian Learning Disabilities Association and is focused on helping students who have learning difficulties at tertiary level.

Learning Difficulties Australia (LDA)
> http://www.ldaustralia.org

LDA is a professional association for educators working with individuals experiencing learning difficulties. Individual student support is provided in some states by qualified special education consultants.

Raising Children Network
> http://www.raisingchildren.net.au/articles/learning_disabilities.html

This Australian Government site has information for parents regarding recognising and supporting children who have learning disabilities/dyslexia.

Royal Children's Hospital Learning Differences Centre
> http://www.rch.org.au/learndiff/index.cfm?doc_id=3563

This centre undertakes assessments for learning disabilities/dyslexia.

Vision Australia Library
> http://www.visionaustralia.org.au/info.aspx?page=514

The Vision Australia site provides information and reading in accessible formats for people across Australia with a print disability.

Materials websites

Quantum Technology
> http://www.quantumrlv.com.au/Learning-Disability-Software.html

Quantum Technology is a company that specialises in inclusive learning technologies, including for people with dyslexia (e.g. text-to-speech and speech-to-text software).

Spectronics
> http://www.spectronicsinoz.com/reading-and-writing-difficulties

Spectronics is a company that specialises in inclusive learning technologies including for people with dyslexia (e.g. text-to-speech and speech-to-text software). This company also has literacy and mathematics support software.

US and UK websites

British Dyslexia Association
> http://www.bdadyslexia.org.uk/

This site has many resources including on creating 'dyslexia friendly' schools and workplaces.

Dyslexia Teacher

http://www.dyslexia-teacher.com/

This site has a free email newsletter, as well as lots of other useful information.

LDOnline

http://www.ldonline.org/

This US learning disabilities site has extensive learning disabilities/dyslexia information and resources for teachers and parents.

LDSuccess

http://www.Ldsuccess.org

This site has a free parent guide to help develop the success attributes of students who have learning difficulties. This has been developed from the long-term studies of successful people who have learning disabilities/dyslexia. There is also a teacher guide (see 'Publications' above).

National Center for Learning Disabilities (NCLD)

http://www.ncld.org/

NCLD is a US-based organisation that works to improve outcomes for children and adults with learning difficulties. Activities include advocacy, provision of accurate information and development and dissemination of educational programs.

Sparktop

http://www.sparktop.com/

Sparktop is a website that was created for children and especially for those who have learning disabilities/dyslexia. It assumes that many such children are very clever and creative. It provides games and activities and features messages from successful people who have dyslexia.